Early Christianity
and Greek Paideia

WERNER JAEGER

Early Christianity
and Greek Paideia

THE BELKNAP PRESS OF
HARVARD UNIVERSITY PRESS

Cambridge, Massachusetts
London, England

Library of Congress Cataloging-in-Publication Data

Jaeger, Werner Wilhelm, 1888–1961.
Early Christianity and Greek Paideia.

Originally published: Cambridge: Belknap Press
of Harvard University Press, 1961
Bibliography: p.
Includes index.
1. Christianity and other religions — Greek — Addresses, essays, lectures.
2. Hellenism — Addresses, essays, lectures.
3. Education, Greek — Addresses, essays, lectures.
4. Greece — Religion — Addresses, essays, lectures.   I.   Title.
BR128.G8J3   1985   270.1   85-8509
ISBN 0-674-22052-8

Preface

The present volume contains the Carl Newell Jackson Lectures for the year 1960, which I had the honor to deliver at Harvard University. Professor Carl Jackson, after whom this lectureship is named, was instrumental in bringing me to Harvard, and it has deep meaning for me to be able to record my lasting gratitude to this man at the moment at which I am retiring from my activity as a teacher in this university.

I have discussed various aspects of the subject of the lectures more briefly on other occasions. The lectures appear here greatly expanded and accompanied by ample notes, which are an essential part of the book; but even in their present enlarged form the lectures are not the full realization of my original plan. When I wrote my *Paideia*, I had intended from the beginning that that work should include a special volume on the reception of the Greek paideia into the early Christian world. But though most of my work since then has been done in the field of ancient Christian literature, it has been precisely the large scope of this work that has prevented my carrying out the plan of a more comprehensive book on the historical continuity and transformation of the tradition of Greek paideia in the Christian centuries of late antiquity. At my present age I can no longer be sure that I shall ever be in a position to treat the issue on that broad scale, and even though I have not given up hope of achieving that goal, now that I think I am sufficiently prepared to do so, I have decided to lay down certain main outlines in these lectures and to publish them as a kind of down payment on what I hope will be a larger whole.

At the moment when, by sheer good fortune, rich treasures of Oriental origin such as the Qumram Scrolls of the Dead Sea and the whole corpus of gnostic writings found at Nag-Hammadi in Upper Egypt have fallen into our hands, and there is a sudden resurgence of historical research on early Christianity, it is inevitable that simultaneously there should begin a total reappraisal of the third great factor that determined the history of the Christian religion — Greek culture and philosophy — in the first centuries of our era. I submit this little book as a first contribution to such a fresh approach.

WERNER JAEGER

Harvard University
Easter 1961

Early Christianity
and Greek Paideia

I

In these lectures I shall not undertake to contrast religion and culture as two heterogeneous forms of the human mind, as might appear from the title, especially in our day, when theologians such as Karl Barth and Brunner insist on the fact that religion is not a subordinate part of civilization, as the old school of liberal theologians often took for granted when they talked of art, science, and religion in one breath. In other words, I do not wish to debate the issue of religion and culture in the abstract, but shall speak of Christianity and its relation to Greek culture quite concretely; and my approach to the phenomenon will be a historical one, as befits the classical scholar. I do not want, either, to compare the Hellenic mind, as it is expressed in the tragedies of Sophocles or in the Parthenon, with the spirit of the Christian faith, as Ernest Renan once did when, returning from his visit to the Holy Land, he set foot on the Acropolis of Athens. He felt overwhelmed by that sublime manifestation of pure beauty and pure reason, as he understood and praised it in his enthusiastic prayer on the Acropolis.[1]

3

Friedrich Nietzsche, his younger contemporary, himself the son of a Protestant minister and a fervent apostle of Dionysus, carried this comparison to an extreme, and from a classical scholar became a missionary of the Antichrist. Instead, I shall speak of Greek culture as it was at the time when the Christian religion appeared and of the historical encounter of these two worlds during the first centuries of our era. The limited space at my disposal will make it impossible for me to speak of early Christian art or to include the Latin hemisphere of late ancient civilization and of the early church.

Ever since the awakening of modern historical consciousness in the second half of the eighteenth century, theological scholars have been aware, when analyzing and describing the great historical process that began with the birth of the new religion, that among the factors that determined the final form of the Christian tradition Greek civilization exercised a profound influence on the Christian mind.[2] Originally Christianity was a product of the religious life of late Judaism.[3] Recent discoveries such as that of the so-called Dead Sea scrolls have cast new light on this period of Jewish religion, and parallels have been drawn between the ascetic piety of the religious sect living at that time on the shores of the Dead Sea and the messianic message of Jesus. There are apparently some striking similarities. But one is struck by one great difference, and that is the fact that the Christian *kerygma* did not stop at the Dead Sea or at the border of Judaea but overcame its exclusiveness and local isolation and penetrated the surrounding world, which was a world unified and dominated by Greek civilization and by the Greek language. This was the decisive fact in the development of the Christian mission and its expansion in and beyond Palestine. It was preceded by three centuries of world-wide expansion of Greek civilization during the Hellenistic period, which was long neglected by classical scholars because they refused to look beyond the classical age of Greece. The great historian who became the discoverer of the period of Greek world-expansion, Johann Gustav Droysen, who was the first to write its history,[4] was motivated, as we now read in his published correspondence, by his Christian faith and dogma, because he had perceived that without this postclassical evolution of Greek culture the rise of a Christian world-religion would have been impossible.[5] Of course, this process of the Christianization of the Greek-speaking world within the Roman Empire was by no means one-sided, for at the same time it meant the Hellenization of the Christian religion. What we have to understand by Hellenization is not clear immediately. Let us try to be more specific.

In the apostolic age we observe the first stage of Christian Hellenism in the use of the Greek language, which we find in the writings of the New Testament,

5

and this continues in postapostolic times, the time of the so-called Apostolic Fathers. This is the original meaning of the word *Hellenismos*.[6] The language question was by no means an irrelevant matter. With the Greek language a whole world of concepts, categories of thought, inherited metaphors, and subtle connotations of meaning enters Christian thought. The obvious explanation of the rapid assimilation of Christianity to its surroundings from the very first generation is of course (1) that Christianity was a Jewish movement, and the Jews were Hellenized by the time of Paul, not only in the Jewish Diaspora but to a considerable extent also in Palestine [7] itself; and (2) that it was precisely this Hellenized portion of the Jewish people to whom the Christian missionaries turned first. It was that part of the Jerusalem community of the apostles called the "Hellenists" in the sixth chapter of Acts which, after the martyrdom of their leader Stephen, was scattered all over Palestine and started the missionary activities of the next generation.[8] Like Stephen himself (Stephanos), they all had good Greek names such as Philippos, Nikanor, Prochoros, Timon, Parmenas, Nikolaos, and mostly they stemmed from Jewish families that had been Hellenized for at least a generation or more.[9] The name of the new sect, Christianoi, originated in the Greek city of Antioch, where these Hellenized Jews found the first great field of activity for their Christian mission.[10] Greek was spoken in the *synagogai* all around the Mediterranean, as is evident from the example of Philo of Alexandria, who did not write his literary Greek for an audience of gentiles but for his highly educated fellow Jews. A large following of gentile proselytes would not have developed had they not been able to understand the language spoken at the Jewish worship in the synagogues of the dispersion. Paul's entire missionary activity was based on this fact. His discussions with the Jews to whom he addressed himself on his travels and to whom he tried to bring the gospel of Christ were carried on in Greek and with all the subtleties of Greek logical argumentation. Both parties as a rule quoted the Old Testament not from the Hebrew original but from the Greek translation of the Septuagint.[11]

Apart from the new form of the Logia, collections of sayings of Jesus, and the Evangelia, the Christian writers of the apostolic age used the Greek literary forms of the Epistle, after the model of Greek philosophers,[12] and the Acts or *Praxeis*, the deeds and teachings of wise or famous men told by their disciples. The further development of a Christian literature in the age of the Apostolic Fathers, which followed these lines, added other types such as the Didachē, the Apocalypse, and the Sermon. The latter took over the form of the Diatribe and Dialexis of Greek popular philosophy, which had tried to bring the teachings of Cynics, Stoics, and Epicureans to the people. Even

7

the form of the martyrology was used by pagans in Egypt, where it developed during the religious struggle between the Egyptians and the Jews at the time of the Apostles, before the Christian martyrologia-literature came into existence.[13] We have to reckon with the existence in Hellenistic times of religious tracts as a means of *propaganda fides* of many sects, although these ephemeral productions did not survive. Plato mentions Orphic tracts that were distributed by members of that sect who went from house to house,[14] and Plutarch in his *Precepts for Newly Married People* advises the female part not to admit strangers by the back door who try to smuggle their tracts into the house advertising a foreign religion, since that may estrange her husband.[15] In the Epistle of James we find the phrase, known to us from Orphic religion, "wheel of birth."[16] The author must have picked it up from some Orphic tract of this sort. They all had a certain family resemblance and occasionally borrowed phrases from one another. One of these groups were the so-called Pythagoreans, who preached the "Pythagorean" way of life and used as their symbol a Y, the sign of the crossroad at which a man had to decide which way to take, the good or the bad.[17] In Hellenistic times we have this teaching of the two ways, which of course was very old (it occurs in Hesiod,[18] for example), in a popular philosophical treatise, the *Pinax of Cebes*, which describes a picture of the two ways found among the votive gifts of a temple.[19] It serves as point of departure for a philosophical moral sermon, like the altar of the unknown God, the inscription of which Paul uses in Acts 17 as the subject for his diatribe. The oldest Christian catechism, which was discovered in the nineteenth century and calls itself the Didache of the Twelve Apostles, offers this same teaching of the two ways as the essence of Christian doctrine, which it combines with the sacraments of baptism and the eucharist.[20] Obviously they were added as a characteristically Christian element; for the two ways were taken over from some pre-Christian tract. This kind of demiliterature included books with ethical aphorisms, such as the ancient Greek tract of Democritus, the father of atomic philosophy, on *Peace of Mind*. It began by saying, "If you want to enjoy peace of mind, do not get involved in too many activities." The book was very famous and widely read.[21] I was astonished when I found this precept transformed into a Christian command in The Shepherd of Hermas in the following form: "Abstain from many activities and thou wilt never go astray. For those who engage in many actions also make many mistakes, and drawn to their various activities they do not serve their lord." [22] Thus, as Philo used to say, and he knew it from his own experience, "the old coin is put to use again by giving it a new stamp." [23]

Thus it was the early Christian mission that forced

the missionaries or apostles to use Greek forms of literature and speech in addressing the Hellenized Jews to whom they turned first and whom they met in all the great cities of the Mediterranean world. This became all the more necessary when Paul approached the gentiles and began to make converts among them. This protreptic activity itself was a characteristic feature of Greek philosophy in Hellenistic times. The various schools tried to find followers by making protreptic speeches in which they recommended their philosophical knowledge or *dogma* as the only way to happiness. We find this kind of eloquence first in the teaching of the Greek sophists and of Socrates as he appears in the dialogues of Plato.[24] Even the word "conversion" stems from Plato, for adopting a philosophy meant a change of life in the first place.[25] Even though the acceptance of it was motivated differently, the Christian kerygma spoke of the ignorance of men and promised to give them a better knowledge, and, like all philosophies, it referred to a master and teacher who possessed and revealed the truth. This parallel situation of the Greek philosophers and the Christian missionaries led the latter to take advantage of it. The God of the philosophers too was different from the gods of the traditional pagan Olympus, and the philosophic systems of the Hellenistic age were for their followers a sort of spiritual shelter. The Christian missionaries followed in their footsteps, and, if we may trust the reports found in the Acts of the Apostles, they at times even borrowed their arguments from these predecessors, especially when addressing an educated Greek audience.[26]

That was the decisive moment in the encounter of Greeks and Christians. The future of Christianity as a world religion depended on it. The author of Acts saw this clearly when he let the apostle Paul visit Athens, the intellectual and cultural center of the classical Greek world and the symbol of its historical tradition, and preach on that venerable spot, the Areopagus, to an audience of Stoic and Epicurean philosophers, about the unknown God.[27] He quotes the verse of a Greek poet, "We are his offspring"; his arguments are largely Stoic and calculated to convince an educated philosophical mind.[28] Whether this unforgettable scene is historical or was meant to dramatize the historical situation of the beginning intellectual struggle between Christianity and the classical world, the setting of the stage reveals clearly how the author of Acts understood it.[29] This discussion required a common basis, else no discussion would be possible. As such a basis Paul chose the Greek philosophical tradition, which was the most representative part of that which was alive in Greek culture at the time. A later Christian writer, the author of the Acts of the Apostle Philip, has interpreted the intention of Acts in the same way: imitating our canonical Acts of the

Apostles, he makes his protagonist come to Athens, like Paul, and speak to the same kind of audience on the same question. He makes the apostle Philip say, "I have come to Athens in order to reveal to you the paideia of Christ." That was indeed what the author of our Acts wanted to do.[30] In calling Christianity the paideia of Christ, the imitator stresses the intention of the apostle to make Christianity appear to be a continuation of the classical Greek paideia, which it would be logical for those who possessed the older one to accept. At the same time he implies that the classical paideia is being superseded by making Christ the center of a new culture. The ancient paideia thereby becomes its instrument.

II

THE oldest datable literary document of Christian religion soon after the time of the apostles is the letter of Clement of Rome to the Corinthians, written in the last decade of the first century. It is interesting to observe the change the Christian mind has undergone in the thirty years since the death of Paul, who had himself written to the same Corinthian church in order to settle disputes among its factions and differences in their interpretations of the Christian faith. Now a powerful group in Corinth had refused to recognize the authority of their bishop, and the church there was in open disagreement. Clement, bishop of Rome, addresses the Corinthians in his capacity as representative of the church that enjoyed the greatest authority.[1] In the manner of ancient rhetorical art he proves to them by many well-chosen examples (*hypodeigmata*) the tragic effects of party strife (*stasis*) and disobedience, and he contrasts with them the blessings of concord and obedience, which he properly divides, like a second Demosthenes, into examples drawn from the remote past and others from more recent times known to his readers from their own experience.[2] When he comes to the point where, according to rhetorical precepts, the most terrifying *topos* was to be added, that internal discord had overthrown great kings and destroyed powerful states, Clement refrains from giving examples, lest he get too deeply involved in secular history, but he is clearly applying the rules of political eloquence. We remember that concord (*homonoia*) had always been the slogan of peacemaking leaders and political educators, of poets, sophists, and statesmen in the classical age of the Greek *polis*.[3] In the Roman period, Concordia had even become a goddess. We see her picture on Roman coins; she is invoked at private wedding ceremonies, at festivals by whole cities, and by the rulers of the

13

Roman Empire. Philosophers had praised her as the divine power that yokes the universe and upholds world order and world peace. So we are not surprised, and yet again we are, when we see Clement refer in that wonderful twentieth chapter of his letter to the cosmic order of all things as the ultimate principle established by the will of God, the creator, as a visible model for human life and peaceful cooperation.

The example of Paul in I Corinthians 12 must have encouraged Clement to recur in this connection to the classical Greek tradition. Paul had told the Corinthians the famous story of the strife that once broke out between the parts of the human body. They refused to fulfill their special functions within the whole organism until they were forced to learn that they are all parts of one body and can exist only as such. It was the fable that Menenius Agrippa told the plebs when they had left the city of Rome and emigrated to the Mons Sacer after deciding that they no longer wanted to live with the patricians; and by it he persuaded them to return. We all know the story from Livy, but it also occurs in several Greek historians.[4] It seems to go back to a Greek sophist's declamation on *Homonoia*.[5] But Clement's proof is different. He lists all the examples of peaceful cooperation in the universe.[6] That argument too we can trace back to Euripides' *Phoinissai*, where Jocasta tries to convince her despotic son Eteocles that peaceful cooperation with the exiled Poly-

nices is the only natural course open to him.[7] Clement
has used a Stoic source for his argument, as is evident
from numerous indications.[8] That source was an enthusiastic praise of peace and harmony as the lord that
rules all nature, beginning with day and night and the
orderly movements of the heavenly bodies and extend-
ing down to the smallest creatures, such as ants and
bees, with their wonderful social community.

It is significant that at that critical moment the
ideals of the political philosophy of the ancient Greek
city-state entered the discussion of the new Christian
type of human community, now called the church, but
in Greek *ekklesia*, which originally meant the assembly
of the citizens of a Greek polis. While at Corinth, then
the capital of the province of Achaia, as Greece was
called in the official language of the Roman administration, all sorts of bearers of the Holy Spirit were
contending with each other, teachers and prophets,
those who knew languages and those speaking in
tongues, that is, ecstatics,[9] it was on the soil of Rome
that a new sense of order was born and made such a
strong appeal to the individualists of the Greek city.[10]
The names of the Roman martyrs Peter and Paul are
invoked by Clement as models of obedience; the
supreme model of submission is Christ himself, but
there is even a reference to the exemplary discipline
of the Roman army.[11] And although Paul's insistence
on faith remains unchanged in Clement's epistle, the

15

special emphasis is on good works, as it is in the Epistle of James, which may belong to the same time and is so clearly polemical against Paul.[12] A whole system of Christian virtues is already emerging from Clement's important historical document; its concept of Christianity is closer to Stoic moralism than to the spirit of St. Paul and his letter to the Romans. That the Christian kerygma should be thus understood and accepted is not surprising, of course. The interpretation of Christianity as essentially an ethical idealism can be found in the New Testament itself throughout the so-called Pastoral Letters. Jewish religion must have favored this kind of interpretation, and even though the principal issue of Paul's generation, the Hebrew ritual law, was no longer a problem for Clement and his contemporaries, they had the rational moral tendency in common with the Jewish Diaspora.[13]

If we want to characterize the spirit of Clement's letter, it is not enough to praise it as an evidence of brotherly love and Christian charity, or to interpret it as an outburst of anger and indignation and as an act of interference in the affairs of the Corinthian church. There is behind it a conception of the church poles apart from that of the Corinthians. The long and powerful declarations on concord and unity which we find in the letter of the Roman church reveal the fundamental conviction that the Christian religion, if it wants to form a true community, requires an inner discipline similar to that of the citizens of a well organized state pervaded by one spirit common to all. There is still room for the pluralism of the early Christian local churches, but they cannot simply act as they please. Their freedom of action and behavior is limited by the disapproval of possible excesses felt by the Christian sister churches at other places and expressed publicly by one of them, one of recognized spiritual and moral authority. It is taken for granted in the letter that the Corinthian anarchy calls for such public admonition, but it is also taken for granted that there exists no other authority in the Christian world that might claim the right to act as the public voice in this situation except the church at Rome.

The letter is impersonal. Clement's name does not occur in it, but is preserved along with the inscription of the letter in our manuscript tradition, and he is quoted as the author by the Corinthians themselves and their bishop Dionysius not long after it, about 170 A.D. Parts of the letter were still read at the divine service in Corinth during the next generations. But Clement avoids appearing in the letter as an author and an individuality; that goes well with the lesson he is teaching the Corinthians about public discipline and order in the Christian church.

The way in which he establishes his concept of order and peace in the human community of the church reveals that it is based on conscious philosophical reflection on the general problem involved. The mere repetition of the emotional appeal to the *agapé* or charity (I Corinthians 13) of which the Corinthians show such a complete lack would not help much, Clement seems to feel. That sort of appeal must have been made many times already by their former leaders. But since they are, at least in part, educated persons and have Greek paideia, he gives his emphasis on civic order in the Christian *politeia* a twofold philosophical background: that of political experience and social ethics and that of cosmological philosophy. The same had been done in Greek paideia, which had always derived its norms of human and social behavior from the divine norms of the universe, which were called "nature" (*physis*). Christian interpreters (and not only they!) ought to remember that this Greek concept of nature is not identical with naturalism in our modern sense, but almost the opposite of it. It is not only in the famous chapter 20 of the letter that we find this cosmic aspect of the problem of peace in the human world placed before the eyes of the readers. In the following chapters the same perspective is maintained throughout, even though it is always combined with the practical application of this point of view to the present case. This does not make the reflections on the principles less philosophical in the eyes of a Greek, for theory and life must always go together, and only when they are understood in this way can the philosopher maintain his claim of imparting the true paideia.

At this point again Clement recurs to the tradition of classical paideia in which he is so well grounded. The organic conception of society which he takes over from Greek political thought acquires in his hands an almost mystical meaning when he interprets it in his Christian manner as the unity of the body of Christ. This mystic idea of the church, which stems from Paul, is filled by Clement with the wisdom of Greek political experience and speculation. After pointing in chapter 37 to the parallel of the Roman army and its hierarchic discipline, which was the object of much wonder and curiosity on the part of the non-Roman population of the Empire (one remembers the long descriptions of the organization and invincible power of the Roman army in Polybius, who speaks about it to the Greeks, and in Josephus, who tells the Jews), Clement goes back to Greek tragedy and quotes Sophocles or Euripides, perhaps taking the words from a Greek philosophical source: the great ones cannot exist without the small, and the small cannot be without the great. Sophocles had taught that in the famous chorus of his *Ajax* (158), but this experience appears in Clement coupled with the general statement that this is so because there is a proper mixture in all things, which makes their practical use possible. The combination of this idea with that of the mutual cooperation of the big and the small in human society is not found in Sophocles' *Ajax*, but it does occur in a similar fragment (21) from Euripides' *Aiolos*, as has been observed by scholars who took such seemingly small things seriously enough to spend their time and labor on them. Their findings are important for our attempt to determine the presence of a living tradition of Greek paideia in the Greek-speaking Christian community at Rome. It spoke Greek because it consisted of Hellenized Jews from the beginning till the end of the first century, and even longer than that. So they could offer the Corinthians their Christian criticism in the language of their classical education. It was for them not only a matter of style, but implied that sort of theoretical generality of intellectual approach to every problem which is the distinctive mark of the Greek paideia.

The Greek word which we have translated by "proper mixture" is a special kind of mixture, which the Greek language calls *krasis* and so distinguishes from a mere juxtaposition of mixed elements without their mutual penetration (in Greek *mixis*). The word used by both Clement and Euripides in this context is a compound of *krasis*, *synkrasis*, which stresses the idea of mutual penetration even more strongly than the simple noun. We therefore ought to translate it by "blend." It was a word of an almost technical meaning, which had a long and interesting history. It was

20

used early in Greek medical thought to mean a thing that, though composed of two or more elements, has coalesced into an indissoluble and well balanced unity. Political and social thinkers came to use the word in order to describe their ideal of political unity as a healthy blend of different social elements in the polis. It was applied also to the cosmos and the unity and order of its elements or parts. In other words, the unity of the church which Clement has in mind and advocates corresponds to that Greek philosophical ideal, and he can explain it most easily by recurring to this analogy, even though Christian religion fills the ancient concept with a new spirit of its own. But it appears on this occasion that, as the Greek mind when it had to deal with the problem of the structure of human society had to go back from the special instance to the phenomenon at large, so the Christian problem of the structure of the new community of the church compels Clement to go back to the general problem as elucidated by Greek philosophy. This repeats itself all the time in the history of Christianity, in the way the classical heritage is incorporated in the structure of Christian thought. It is not only as an element of dogmatic theology that it later enters the Christian mind; it is there from the very beginning in a very practical form, inseparable from life itself.

Clement goes on to say that this unity which he has illustrated first by the order of the Roman army and

21

then by the analogy of the great and the small in the organism of human society is a natural one, which he compares to the relation of the human body and its parts. He quotes here the apostle Paul (I Corinthians 12.21–22), who had been the first Christian teacher to point out this ideal, and who used it as the framework for his famous message of Christian *agapé*. Clement does not repeat the moving details of Paul's hymn on *agapé*, which the Corinthians of course knew by heart. He only stresses the importance of the smallest parts of the human body for the life of the whole body, and triumphantly ends up his argument, at the close of chapter 37, with the assertion that "they all breathe together" (Greek *sympnei*, Latin *conspirant*) and by doing so subordinate themselves to the preservation of the whole body. Again we have here one of those truly Greek concepts which became fundamental and characteristic of a whole philosophy. The verb *sympneo* means having a common *pneuma* or spirit. The fact that Clement uses this word of the parts of the body implies that one pneuma permeates and animates the whole organism of the body. This idea came from Greek medicine [14] and from there was taken over by Stoic philosophy. What was meant originally as an explanation of organic life in the human body was now transferred to the life in the universe: it was all permeated by the life-giving pneuma, according to the Stoic theory of *physis*. The *sympnoia* of the parts,

22

which the physicians had stated with regard to the body of man, now was made the principle of the living universe and became a *sympnoia pantōn*. From the Stoic cosmology we can trace this idea through the philosophy of Neoplatonism down to Leibniz. And this concept Clement uses to illustrate his ideal of the spiritual unity of the Church. The Christian notion of the "holy pneuma" may have prompted him to accept the idea more readily. At any rate, it is one of those metaphorical concepts that have proved applicable to the most heterogeneous things. Both the idea of *synkrasis* and that of *sympnoia* belong together and reveal their origin from the same philosophical source, which was concerned with the problem of political harmony in human society. Clement needed it for his purpose of establishing firmly in the rapidly growing church the ideal of an *ordo Christianus*, which assigns to each member of this community his own place and way of cooperating according to his ability. There is a special place and function for the high priest and his service, and another for the priests, another for the levites and deacons, another one for the layman. Each of them is not to exceed the limit of his service, but must be contented with it. These examples are taken by Clement from the Jewish law and its tradition in the Scriptures. They are not literally transferable to the church, but obviously tend to become the pattern of its new hierarchy.

The authority assumed in the letter by those who are talking to the Corinthian church rests on the hypothesis that this is not an act of arrogance on the part of the Roman church, but the fulfillment of their duty as Christians toward their brothers whom they see go astray. In the conclusion of the letter, immediately preceding the solemn and beautiful prayer with which it ends, Clement once more gives deterring examples, taken from both the Scripture and pagan history (as he expressly states in chapter 55). Then he turns to the praise of paideia, thereby defining his entire epistle as an act of Christian education. This must have appeared to him as the true justification of his initiative, and it must have cast its light also backwards on the letters of the apostles which later were to be collected as part of a "New Testament." No wonder that his epistle to the Corinthians for centuries belonged to that group of books. To a man of Greek education the word paideia must have suggested itself most naturally for what he was trying to achieve by his letter. The biblical authority for this — their Bible still being our Old Testament — was not missing either, and is abundantly quoted in the concluding part of his epistle. The Septuagint often speaks of paideia; there it still means what the Hebrew original understood in these passages quoted by Clement: the chastisement of the sinner that brings about a change of mind in him. For Clement also,

24

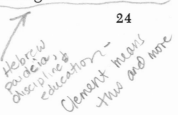

this old meaning of the word is always present. But it is clear that he applies it in a much wider sense in his letter and, while using the scriptural testimony, he himself conceives of paideia as precisely that which he offers to the Corinthians in his whole letter. In that sense the letter to the Ephesians, and some other passages in the apostolic writings which were in high esteem at his time in the Christian churches, spoke of the *paideia tou kyriou*, and that is the word Clement must have in mind when he speaks in several passages toward the end of his letter of the "paideia of God" or the "paideia of Christ" as the great protective force in the life of the Christian.[15] There can be no doubt that what he takes over in his letter from a great philosophical tradition and from other pagan sources is included by him in this comprehensive concept of the divine paideia, for if this were not so, he could not have used it for his purpose in order to convince the people at Corinth of the truth of his teachings. These general truths and statements of Greek poets and thinkers which he incorporates in his Christian paideia are meant as corroborative evidence, and stress the character of his work as paideia. This way of presenting his own "advice" is meant to make it more easily acceptable to the misled Corinthian brethren. As a lasting code of that new paideia the document survived the situation for which it was written. It is due to this conception the author had of his own work that even in the final prayer he gives thanks to God for sending us Christ, "through whom Thou hast educated and sanctified us and honored us." The high evaluation of paideia in this last part of the letter, in which Clement tries to make the addressees understand the purpose (*skopos*) of his writing, cannot be explained entirely by the role the idea had played until then in Christian thought; it is without doubt enhanced by the great value given it by its use in Greek civilization.

III

THE earlier Christian literature is meant for Christians and those on the way to adopting the Christian religion. It is so far an internal affair of the Christian community. But the immediate reason for Christian writers to address themselves to a non-Christian audience was the cruel persecution to which followers of Christ were subjected everywhere in the Roman Empire. Thus there came into existence, about the middle of the second century, a large body of literature through which Christians spoke to the pagan majority of the population in self-defense. It is obvious that this polyphonic chorus could not in their apology take for granted what they were going to defend. That is what distinguished their situation from earlier Christian literature. These new advocates of their religion had to find some common ground with the people they addressed if they wanted to reach an understanding. That compelled them to take a more rational approach to their own cause, in order to make it possible for others to join them in a real discussion. Most of them chose a didactic form of speech, answering possible objections or slander, but the situation itself led to a revival of the dialogue form as we find it in Justin Martyr's dialogue with Trypho, which is a classic example not of external imitation of a rigidified literary pattern but of a true effort by the partners in the dialogue to understand each other instead of asking questions only for the sake of refutation.[1] This attempt could be made only in the atmosphere of Greek intellectual culture. The language is therefore different in tone from the older enthusiastic Christian eloquence. The writers do not undertake to speak to the illiterate masses, but write for people who read for the purpose of obtaining better information. They speak to the educated few, including the rulers of the Roman Empire.[2] They address them individually as men of higher culture (paideia), who will approach such a problem in a philosophical spirit.[3] And that is not just flattery: no ruler on earth deserved such a characterization more than a Hadrian, an Antoninus Pius, or a Marcus Aurelius, to whom some of these works are dedicated. Christians had to face the accusation of outright cannibalism because in the eucharist they ate the flesh and drank the blood of their God. They were called atheists because they did not worship the gods of the state. They denied divine honor to the emperor himself, so their atheism was at the same time political subversion.[4]

The defense of Christianity had to employ philosophical arguments throughout. Had not the great philosophers Socrates and Plato and many others taught the same thing?[5] Disbelief in the gods of the old poets and the popular religion was as old as philosophy itself.[6] And had not Socrates already suffered the death of a martyr for his purer concept of the Divine?[7] He was the prototype of the suffering just, a true *typos*, like some of the figures of the Old Testament who were supposed to point forward to the coming of Christ. The Stoics had taught that the divine principle and cause of the world was the Logos, which penetrated all that exists. This Logos, which Socrates had partly anticipated, had taken on human form in Christ, as the fourth gospel says, for Christ there appears as the creative power of the Word through which the world was made.[8] Justin tells in his dialogue how he had been drawn to Greek philosophy from his early youth; indeed, he had studied one of its systems after another, since none of them completely satisfied him, until he found his final answer in the Christian religion.[9] But even after becoming a Christian he did not take off the mantle of the Greek philosopher, because Christianity to him meant the absolute philosophy.[10] The whole issue is a philosophical problem not only for Justin but for his contemporaries at large.

The interpretation of Christianity as a philosophy should not surprise us, for when we stop to consider for a moment with what a Greek could compare the phenomenon of Jewish-Christian monotheism we find nothing but philosophy in Greek thought that corresponds to it. Indeed, when the Greeks met the Jewish religion for the first time in Alexandria in the third century B.C., not long after Alexander the Great, the Greek authors who give us their first impressions of their encounter with the Jewish people, such as Hecataeus of Abdera, Megasthenes, and Clearchus of Soli on Cyprus, the pupil of Theophrastus, invariably speak of the Jews as a "philosophical race." [11] What they mean of course is that the Jews had always held certain views about the oneness of the divine principle of the world at which Greek philosophers had arrived only quite recently. Philosophy had served as a platform for the first attempts at a closer contact of East and West at the time when Greek civilization began to move eastward under Alexander and probably even earlier than that. The Jew mentioned in the lost dialogue of Clearchus, who met Aristotle during the years when he was teaching at Assos in Asia Minor, is described as a perfect Greek not only in his language but also in his soul.[12] What is a "Greek soul" in the eyes of a Peripatetic scholar? Not what modern historical or philological scholarship tries to grasp in Homer, Pindar, or in Periclean Athens, of course; a Greek soul is for him the intellectualized human mind in whose crystal-clear world even a highly gifted and intelligent foreigner could participate and move with perfect ease and grace. Perhaps they could never understand each other in their ultimate motivation, perhaps the intellectual ear of each did not perceive the fine overtones in the language of the other; but enough — they thought that they *could* understand each other, and their brave attempts seemed to promise a surprising success. I am afraid the Jewish holy book would never have been translated, and the Septuagint might never have come into existence, were it not for the expectation of the Greeks in Alexandria to find in it the secret of what they respectfully called the philosophy of the barbarians.[13] Behind that venture there is the new idea of the "one humanity" that Alexander had propagated by his policy after he had conquered the Persian Empire.[14]

For us Philo of Alexandria is, of course, the prototype of the Jewish philosopher who has absorbed the entire Greek tradition and makes use of its rich conceptual vocabulary and its literary means in order to prove his point, not to the Greeks but to his own fellow Jews.[15] That is important, since it shows that all understanding, even among non-Greek people, needed the intellectual medium of Greek thought and its categories. It was indispensable in particular for the discussion of religious matters, because philosophy by that time had taken on for the Greeks themselves the function of natural theology.[16] Aristotle, following the strong tendencies of the late Plato, had conceived his "first philosophy" as theology.[17] But the element of philosophical religion, which thus was separated from physics or cosmology, had been there in Greek thought in more or less developed form from the beginning,[18] and since Aristotle had proclaimed its primacy, it can be found in every system of Greek philosophy, Platonic, Stoic, even Epicurean, with the exception only of the Sceptic. In Justin Martyr's dialogue the conversation starts when the Jew Trypho meets [19] the Greek philosopher while taking a walk in the colonnade of a gymnasium.[20] He says to him, "I see you are a philosopher," and assumes he must therefore be concerned with God and the theological problem.[21] This the other man promptly confirms. Thus this idea of a philosopher as a man interested in God was taken for granted in the middle of the second century A.D.

What made Christianity appear as a philosophy at

31

this time was its concern with ethics and cosmology but primarily with theology. This was so not only for a Jewish but also for a pagan observer. That is why Christian views begin to be mentioned in pagan literature about that time. Tacitus had still thought of the Christians as a politically fanatic section of the Jewish people that had carried on the rebellion against the Roman overlords that ended with the destruction of Jerusalem under Titus.[22] Marcus Aurelius still speaks of the Christian martyrs as religious fanatics, whose valor and constancy he would like to admire if he did not despise it as a forced theatrical show.[23] That is how the enthusiastic will to suffer death through the wild beasts in the Coliseum, as we find it expressed in the letters of Ignatius of Antioch,[24] must have affected the melancholy Stoic philosopher on the throne. But another famous contemporary, the pagan physician and philosopher Galen, speaks of Jews and Christians as philosophers. He compares Moses' cosmology with that of Epicurus and Plato, whose *Timaeus* he prefers because Plato does not deal only with the "will" of the creator, the divine fiat, but gives a picture of the divine workmanship that could satisfy the artistic and rational spirit of the Greeks.[25] In speaking of the philosophy of the Christians, Galen criticizes their reliance on "faith," which to him represents mere subjective evidence and indicates the lack of a sufficient epistemological foundation for their system.[26] The problem of faith and reason had not yet been raised, except by a non-Greek Christian apologist, the African Tertullian. In his arguments against the pagan gods and superstitions Tertullian depends entirely on his Greek-Christian predecessors, who had in turn taken their arguments from the Greek philosophers; but he does not share their opinion that Christianity itself is a philosophy.[27] He distinguishes sharply between the faith of the Christian religion and philosophy as a mere rational attitude, and sees the superiority of faith over reason precisely in its suprarational character. In this he foreshadows developments of the Latin form of Christianity, of great importance and quite different from the Greek interpretation. The Greeks always welcome the support of reason, whereas the Roman mind stresses throughout (1) the factor of personality in the acceptance of the Christian faith and (2) the suprapersonal factor of authority.

This basic difference in the Roman and Greek approach to the problem of religious certainty did not first evidence itself when the question of Christianity was under discussion. It already appears with regard to Roman religion and tradition in Cicero's third book *De natura deorum*. After Epicurean and Stoic philosophers have shown what their philosophies have to contribute to the problem, the speaker in book III, who is philosophically a sceptic but at the same time the Pontifex Maximus of the Roman state, rejects their rational arguments on the existence and nature of the gods on principle as subject to logical suspicion, and declares that he is unable to accept them as the basis of his religious conduct. The only basis he can see for it is the acceptance of that religion on which the Roman state is founded, or the authority of the tradition.[28] It has always seemed to me that this Ciceronian solution, truly Roman as it is, anticipates later developments when the same problem returned after the Christian faith had taken the place of the old pagan gods.

Let us now return to the Greek apologists, who were less radical in their doubts about philosophical reason. The only one who shared the suspicion of a Tertullian in the East was the Assyrian Tatian, who wrote Greek like all the others and possessed Greek culture, but who did not believe in it.[29] He violently disapproved of the direction in which the Christian trend of his time was going: he warned Christians that the future of their cause did not lie in their gradual assimilation to Greek culture but would depend entirely on their keeping it immaculately pure as a barbarous cult. Justin appears very cultivated, compared with this champion of anti-Hellenism. Tatian cannot have been an isolated figure. After the eastward advance of Hellenism during the first centuries after Alexander's conquest of Asia, a strong reaction of the East was bound to follow. The advance of Jewish and Christian religion as such was a part of it. But the chances for this unmitigated form of reaction to gain a strong foothold in the countries that had been more deeply penetrated by Hellenic influence were slim, and whenever its hour seems to have arrived, it does not last long. On the other hand, he who has once believed in Plato and Pythagoras as the strong bulwarks of all philosophy and spiritual values, as Justin calls them in his dialogue with the old stranger in the desert,[30] will be led to certain consequences with regard to his views of divine providence in history. Was God revealed only to the Jews in the Law and the Prophets? Had not Paul in his Epistle to the Romans already recognized the contribution made by pagan wisdom to the cause of truth? [31] It is true, he did not recognize it outright as another aspect of God's revelation; but even if one did not go beyond this limited recognition, had the headway made in history by the Greek mind been achieved independently of the educational plan of divine providence? Such were the problems that confronted the advancing Christian movement in the times of the apologists. Through the door that they opened, Greek culture and tradition streamed into the church and became amalgamated with its life and doctrine. The era of the great teachers and thinkers of early Christianity was beginning.

ONE can understand the historical development
of the Christian religion during the first centuries as
a process of continuous "translation" of its sources,
aimed at giving the world an ever more accurate understanding and realization of their content. This process began when the first evangelists, going back to
the earliest extant oral or written reports of the sayings
and doings of Jesus, translated them from the original
Aramaic into Greek and arranged them in their present
form. A further step was taken when a writer like
Luke, with his better education in Greek, found those
early translations defective in language and presentation of the material and tried to adjust their form to
his own higher standards. But translation in that literal
sense was only a first attempt to get at the meaning of
the original words. Soon another kind of explanation
was needed, one that not only gave the very words of
the text tradition but held it imperative to concentrate on the meaning of the Christian message and on
the questions Who was Jesus? and What was his celes-
tial authorization? The interpretations at first operated
within the Jewish categories of the Law and the
Prophets and within the Messianic tradition of Israel;
but soon the attempt was made to adapt them to the

ears and minds of Greek-speaking people in order to make their reception into the Hellenic world possible. The interpretative process was thereby automatically transferred to a higher level, and it took great minds to approach this formidable task.

The apologists of the second century were men of respectable intellectual attainments, but Christianity now needed the services of the more highly developed minds and personalities that were to be found in the cultural environment of Alexandria, capital of the Hellenistic world. East and West had met and vied with one another there ever since Alexander the Great had founded the city. There, in the time of Jesus and Paul, Philo, the Jewish philosopher, tried to demonstrate in numerous works written in Greek that his Hebrew religion could be represented and understood in terms of Greek philosophy, and he so justified it before the judgment of reason. Thus it was not unprecedented when two centuries later the Hellenic and Christian traditions came face to face with one another at this crossroad of history. Thus far they had lived in the same environment in a state of undeclared hostility, and only on occasion had they exchanged views or arguments. That exchange was to be carried on on a larger scale from now on, but on a higher level, as is manifest in the most famous examples of that great controversy between Greek and Christian scholars in the third century, Origen's *Contra Celsum* and the

Neoplatonist Porphyry's great work *Against the Christians*. But these attacks already take for granted the rise in the Christian camp of true Christian scholarship and of a philosophical "theology," a form of the Christian spirit that could hardly develop before the Christian faith and Greek philosophical tradition became embodied in one and the same individual, as they did in the persons of Clement of Alexandria and of Origen, his greater pupil. It was this personal union of both worlds that produced a highly complex synthesis of Greek and Christian thought.

When we try to answer the question why Christianity, which originally was a product of the religious life of late Judaism, underwent this complete transformation, or why ancient Greek culture in the end adopted this Oriental faith that seems so far removed from the classical form of the Greek mind, both classical humanists and Christians face great difficulties. The modern classicist tends to see the Greek heritage as a culture self-sufficient and essentially anthropocentric, and cannot easily understand that apparently, if ever, it no longer was so at the time when Christianity offered its own concept of man and human life to the later generations of "Greek" civilization. He easily forgets that the city of Athens, where Paul when he walked through the streets found at every step the signs of a god-fearing people,[1] had been described in almost the same words by Sophocles in his *Oedipus at*

Colonus; in that city religious feeling had deep roots.[2] Monotheistic ideas had crept into the old faith via a philosophical discussion that at Paul's time had already been going on for centuries and had reached even the ears of the common man.[3] On the other hand, Christians of our own day who possess a definite theology, be it that of Thomas Aquinas or Martin Luther, cannot easily grasp a form of Christian religion that does not yet place its theological emphasis on the same ideas that they themselves deem essential. If we want to attain a genuine understanding of this historical phenomenon, we must not expect to find our own modern one-sided purism, be it humanistic or theological, confirmed in early Greek Christian thought. What we find in history is mostly the precise opposite of that kind of clear-cut logical consistency on which we insist in our theories. In reality the Greek cultural ideals and Christian faith did mix, however anxious we may be to keep each of them immaculate. There was on both sides a powerful desire for mutual penetration, regardless of how reluctant to assimilate these two languages were, each with its different ways of feeling and of metaphorical self-expression. Both sides must finally have come to recognize that, beneath all that, an ultimate unity existed between them, and a common core of ideas, which so sensitive a thinker as Santayana did not hesitate to call "humanistic," though he perhaps did not mean this to be taken as unqualified praise. The product then should not be dismissed as a typical example of that religious syncretism of which there is such an abundance in these early centuries. The interpretation of the religion that had as its symbols the Incarnation and the *Ecce homo* followed an inevitable historical logic. It led to a rebirth of certain basic concepts, the *ideae innatae*, so to speak, of the Greek mind, which must have given it new strength and self-assurance in spite of the external appearance of defeat and radical change. On the other hand, the creative contact of Christianity with these constant ideas of the Greek tradition must have reassured the Christian mind of its own universality (catholicity). This claim had been made by the Christian religion from the very beginning and had been constantly maintained, the claim to be the truth. Such a claim could not fail to measure itself by the only intellectual culture of the world that had aimed at and achieved universality, the Greek culture that was predominant in the Mediterranean world. The dream of Alexander when he founded the city that bears his name was now to be realized: two universal systems, Greek culture and the Christian church, were to be united in the mighty superstructure of Alexandrian theology.

At this juncture the Christian faith begins to participate in the great historical process of the Greek mind and to join in the continuous rhythm of its life. For it would be wrong to think that the Hellenization of Christian thought that we see taking place at that moment was a one-sided process, unrelated to the internal needs of Greek civilization as it itself existed at that moment. The evolution of the Greek mind from the earliest time reveals, after an initial period of mythological thinking, a growing tendency toward rationalization of all forms of human activity and thought. As its supreme manifestation it produced philosophy, the most characteristic and unique form of the Greek genius and one of its foremost titles to historical greatness. The climax of this progressive development was reached in the schools of Plato and Aristotle. The systems of the Stoics and Epicureans that followed them in the early Hellenistic age are an anticlimax and show a decline from their creative philosophical power. Philosophy becomes a set of dogmas, which, though based on a certain conception of the world and of nature, are primarily aimed at guiding human life by the teachings of philosophy and giving it an inner security no longer to be found in the outside world. This kind of philosophy thereby fulfills a religious function. To understand that, one has only to remember the hymn to Zeus of the Stoic Cleanthes or the enthusiastic praise that Lucretius devotes to his master Epicurus and to his doctrine. Both Stoicism and Epicureanism, though opposed to each other in most other respects, have this in com-

41

mon, that they satisfy a nonrational religious need and try to fill a vacuum that was left by the ancient Greek cult-religion of the Olympic gods. But the spirit of cool research and critical analysis of the cognitive faculties of the human mind was still strong enough for the greatest assault ever made by a Greek thinker on this kind of salvational knowledge as principle, and the result was that Greek philosophical thought ended in a heroic scepticism that radically denied all dogmatic philosophy of past and present and, going far beyond that, declared its complete abstention from any positive statement about true and false, not only with regard to metaphysical speculation but with regard to mathematical and physical science as well.

The Greek mind in a way never recovered from the blow, and it did not produce a great philosophy in the old sense after the rise of this *skepsis*. But the traditional philosophical schools gradually undertook a strange sort of self-defense by joining forces and concluding a *grande alliance* to which Platonists, Stoics, Pythagoreans, and (to a lesser degree) Aristotelians made their contribution. This was possible only by neglecting their differences, of which the Sceptics had made much in their polemic, and by trying to find some common ground. In their demands for philosophical certainty they had become very modest. While the old schools still repeated their arguments, Cicero showed in his dialogue *On the Nature of the*

Gods how positive religion, such as the old Roman religious tradition, could profit by the diffident scepticism of Greek philosophers; for, as we have observed, the highly educated Aurelius Cotta prefers being a sceptic philosophically to accepting the rational arguments of Stoic natural theology, whereas in matters of positive religious worship he simply adopts the old Roman tradition as an integral part of the entire political system of the *res publica*.[4] But even wherever philosophers went beyond this limit and maintained a more positive metaphysical position, as did Stoics and Platonists, they too had recourse to the still existent ancient cult religion and to the allegoric interpretation of its myths. They also showed a special interest in the religions of the "barbarians," most of all the Orient, including the Jews and their imageless worship. The technical parts of philosophy became more and more the esoteric knowledge of a few learned commentators whose huge works nobody read.[5] At the time of Cicero, for example, no Greek philosopher (so he says, with probably only slight exaggeration) could read Aristotle.[6] The literary form of philosophic thought had to be made understandable to the reading public; thus the systematic manner of presentation yielded more and more to the essay form or to popular diatribe, and the emphasis was on theological problems. Musonius, Epictetus, Plutarch, Pseudo-Longinus, Dio of Prusa, and the emperor Marcus Aurelius, not to speak of Apollonius of Tyana and similar strange figures, all show this trend, and even the custodians of the tradition of formal classicism like Aelius Aristides felt that their declamations needed religion for a subject, since that was what most people now wanted to hear.[7] Satires were not lacking, but Lucian's sharp taunting is the exception that proves the rule. It gives an extremely lifelike picture of the excesses of contemporary superstition and bigotry.

No wonder then that even the school philosophy of that time followed this general trend. It is reflected most eloquently in the interpretation that the Platonic Academy of the second century A.D., usually referred to as Middle Platonism, gives of Plato's philosophy. It could rightly be said that the great revival of Plato that we see everywhere in the Greek-speaking world of that time was due not so much to the intensification of learned study that accompanied it as to the role of "the divine Plato" as supreme religious and theological authority, a role that he assumed in the course of the second century and that reached its culminating point in the so-called Neoplatonism of Origen's generation in the third century.[8] No mere formal classicism could save that old civilization. The reason for its survival as a whole was the fact that it possessed Plato; had it not been for him, the rest of Hellenic culture might have died along with the old Olympian gods. The Greek humanists understood their situation well enough, and so did the philosophers of the Platonic Academy, who profited by the religious tendency of the period. It would not suffice to compose a new kind of stately prose hymn, as did the rhetor Aristides, in honor of the ancient Greek deities, giving each a philosophical interpretation in the allegoric fashion of the Stoics; so other classicists infused the Greek cultural system with Plato as its living inner fire to lend new warmth and light to the cold marble of the noble forms. What they meant by Plato was not an epistemology or the social theories of his *Republic*, which still retained too much of the tense spirit of the old *polis* state for people who were living as subjects under the peaceful administration of the Roman Empire. Plato's Ideas, which once had been attacked by Aristotle as the substance of his master's philosophy, were now interpreted as the thoughts of God, in order to give Platonic theology a more concrete form.[9] Clement and Origen grew up under this cultural system. It dominated not only the philosophical schools of their time but also the traditional Hellenic paideia. Porphyry, the Syrian Neoplatonist, did not derive his Platonic faith from his philosophical teacher Plotinus, whom later in his life he met in Rome. He acquired it at the very source of classical culture and education, at Athens, in the school of the rhetorician Longinus, who, according to Plotinus, was not a philosopher at all

but the greatest philologue of his age.[10] Both philology
and philosophy were tending in the same direction.
They began their teaching with Homer but ended it
with Plato, whose dialogues they read and explained.[11]
They led their pupils the way to that spirituality which
was the common link of all higher religion in late antiquity. From this source of religious feeling all the
traditions, pagan and Christian, were reinterpreted to
make them acceptable to the men of the new age. They
began to remember that it had been Plato who made
the world of the soul visible for the first time to the
inner eye of man, and they realized how radically that
discovery had changed human life. So, on their way
upward, Plato became the guide who turned their
eyes from material and sensual reality to the imma-
terial world in which the nobler-minded of the human
race were to make their home.

V

In this situation Clement of Alexandria, the head
of the Christian school of the Catechetes, and Origen
became the founders of Christian philosophy. It was
not a complete system comprising all disciplines, such

as logic, physics, and ethics, in the Aristotelian or Stoic manner, but it consisted exclusively in what these earlier pagan thinkers had called theology. Thus theology as such was not what was new in the philosophical thought of the Alexandrians.[1] New was the fact that philosophical speculation was used by them to support a positive religion that was not itself the result of independent human search for the truth, like earlier Greek philosophies, but took as its point of departure a divine revelation contained in a holy book, the Bible. Even that was not quite without precedent, for Philo, as we have seen, had done something similar with the Jewish religion, and in Greek philosophy the Stoics had interpreted the old Greek myths allegorically. Aristotle himself had declared that the ancient gods of Greek popular religion were the same thing as the theology of his unmoved mover, only expressed in mythical form,[2] just as he taught that Hesiod's theogony was a *sophizesthai* in mythical form.[3] The Alexandrian interpretation of the Bible, especially that of Origen, applied this method systematically to the sources of the Christian religion, just as his pagan fellow-Platonists in the schools of Longinus and Plotinus used it for their explanation of Homer, as we learn from Porphyry's *Homeric Questions*.[4] Behind this phenomenon there lies, as concerns pagan tradition, the strong conservatism of Greek philosophical rationalism with its wish to preserve the whole tradition of the prerational layers of the Greek mind. Plato in his *Republic* had rejected Homer and Hesiod not as poetic fiction but as paideia, which for him meant the expression of truth.[5] Against him the Stoic school had maintained Homer and Hesiod as normative expressions of the truth in order to retain the old poetry as the basis of Greek paideia. Therefore they had to create a whole system of allegoric meaning, which they sought in the mythical stories. It was in the first place done for theological reasons, in order to protect the oldest written tradition of the Greeks against the accusation of blasphemy.[6] In the same way the Alexandrians wanted to save the Old Testament from those radical critics who rejected it and wished to get rid of it altogether; this they achieved, in Origen's theology, by the distinction of a literal, a historical, and a spiritual meaning of the texts. This made it possible for them to avoid the philosophical objection of crude anthropomorphism in the way in which God is represented in the Old Testament. The anthropomorphic character of the gods of the Greek myths had been from the beginning the point against which Greek philosophy had directed its attacks. It began with Xenophanes of Colophon, who criticized the gods of Homer and Hesiod as all too human and as lacking the dignity that befits the divine nature. Later Greek thinkers called this *theoprepés*, and this word runs like a leitmotiv through the history

of Greek philosophical theology.[7] Origen's controversy
with Celsus shows that this was the fundamental criticism that contemporary pagan philosophers launched
against the Christian doctrine — its mythological character. So Origen set out on his lifelong attempt to
translate the Bible from the level of its literal meaning
to that of its spiritual sense. He thus saved what we
might call the Christian paideia and its foundation in
the Bible, as the Stoics had done with Homer's theology. He commented on almost all the important books
of the Old Testament and much of the New Testament,
combining his philosophical theology with the closest
philological study of the sacred texts, which he re-
constituted in his monumental work, the *Hexapla*.

What is the function of philosophy in Origen's
theological method? It is obvious that he makes use
of it throughout his reading of the Scriptures. It is
not only an abstract dogmatic system separate from
his exegesis, but penetrates his whole understanding
of the religion of Jesus and the Apostles, transforming
it into theology in the Greek manner. His is a complicated mind. He is perfectly able to read his Bible
like a child and enjoy it in the simplicity of a humble
heart, as we see when we read his sermons in which
he speaks to plain folk without making much use of
all his learning.[8] So a great astronomer, engaged all
day long in his complicated mathematical reckonings,
may still be able to look up to the stars in the quiet

of the night and enjoy their beauty without reference to his normal apparatus of telescopes and arithmetical formulae. But Origen taught philosophy in its pure form also. He had to do so, because his philosophical thought always took as point of departure the great historical systems of the past and the texts of the philosophers themselves. We happen to be well-informed about the manner of his teaching, since we can still read the reports about it that both his enemies and his admiring students have left to us.

Origen owed his culture to Greek philosophy. Porphyry, the Neoplatonist, has given us a very revealing picture of the great Christian Platonist, who must have fascinated the pagan Platonists of his time, but who by the same token must have been a great scandal to them. Porphyry had seen the famous man when he himself was still quite young. He formulates the paradox of Origen's double life in saying that Origen, though brought up as a Greek in Greek letters, nevertheless became a proponent of that barbarous enterprise, Christianity. But though he lived the life of a Christian, he held Hellenic views about all things, including God, and he gave all the foreign myths a Greek meaning. For he lived with Plato constantly and read the entire literature of the Platonists and Pythagoreans of the preceding generation. But then, Porphyry continues, he reads all the mysteries of the Greeks into the Jewish writings (he is referring to Origen's commentaries on the various books of the Old Testament).[9] This picture of Origen's relation to philosophy is confirmed by one of Origen's pupils, the Cappadocian Gregory Thaumaturgus, who later became the apostle of his Cappadocian homeland and thereby was the link between Origen and the Cappadocian fathers Basil, Gregory Nazianzen, and Gregory of Nyssa, all of whom were great readers and admirers of Origen. The Thaumaturg gave a farewell address to Origen when he left after five years of study with him during Origen's exile in Palestine. In it he tells that the master urged his pupils to acquaint themselves with every Greek philosophy, and that he instructed them himself as a critical exegete. He took them on a long intellectual journey, always eliminating that which seemed sophistic and weak and laying before them what in his opinion was good and sound.[10]

That is the method of teaching which was used in the schools of Greek philosophy and still is in our own day, because philosophy by its very nature has its existence in its own great history, far more so than any mere science. We find the same method in the writings of Plotinus that reflect his own teaching. There he often raises a problem taken from one of the earlier philosophers, particularly Plato and Aristotle, who were read in the schools. How they were read we learn from the preserved commentaries of the later Platonists such as Iamblichus, Simplicius, and Proclus.[11]

The words of Porphyry leave no doubt that Origen
devoted a lifelong study to the important philosophers
of the past and that he had a vast knowledge of the
rich special literature about Plato in monographic
form.[12] Porphyry's report might give the impression
that this knowledge appeared mostly when Origen
was interpreting the books of the Scriptures, but what
Gregory Thaumaturgus says about the master's insistence upon the study of "all the philosophers" seems
to prove that he also taught philosophy separately,
apart from his biblical lectures and for its own sake.
By such courses in philosophy Porphyry may have
been attracted to the biblical ones, but he was dis-
appointed there by the allegorical method that he himself later applied to the exegesis of Homer.[13] On the
Christian side criticism was not lacking either, and the
school of Antioch interpreted the Bible more literally
and historically. But the Cappadocian fathers of the
Church followed Origen's method, and so did many
others among the Christian theologians, regardless of
whether they accepted all of Origen's special interpretations or not. What seemed to them to justify their
kind of approach to this problem was the fact that this
allegorical method had already been used by the biblical authors in some instances, even by the apostle Paul
himself. It must go back to the rabbinical school of his
time, and it is hard to imagine indeed how they could
have dealt with a book like the Song of Songs without

explaining it allegorically. Among the works of the so-called Apostolic Fathers the Epistle of Barnabas had advanced in this direction.[14] But the new theology of the Alexandrians went much further in the systematic use of this method, and authors like Origen and, following his example, Gregory of Nyssa insisted that even the historical books of the Old Testament were to be understood in this way, that is, as transparent illustrations of great metaphysical or ethical truths.[15] This was to them a striking proof of the pedagogy of the Holy Spirit.

The distinction between the "simpler" Christian minds of mere "believers" and the theologian who "knows" the true meaning of the holy books is common to both Clement and Origen and followed with inevitable logic from their treatment of the Scriptures.[16] In this regard too they must have had predecessors in the Christian tradition itself. *Gnosis* is the fashionable word for this trend to transcend the sphere of *pistis*, which in Greek philosophical language always had the connotation of the subjective. Such a distinction occurs as early as in the letters of Paul, whatever was its exact meaning. The tendency became stronger in the second century, when whole systems that call themselves "gnostic" appear. Their teachings were very different. Those which had anything to do with Christianity had in common the trend to find a secret in the Scriptures. Others recurred in part to a fantastic mythological speculation about the various stages of the cosmic process, including views of the human soul and its destiny. It is not possible in this connection to speculate about gnosis and its historical origin at a moment when a large corpus of gnostic source material has just been discovered, material that has not even been edited yet but that may change the traditional picture of this religious phenomenon.[17] But its mere existence in the second and third centuries is sufficient proof that there must have been some need for this strange sort of religious ersatz, since its dispersion was so rapid and widespread in the Roman Empire.

The strong emphasis on gnosis in Clement and Origen shows that they had to pay attention to this new power that threatened to become a dangerous rival of Christianity, to be reckoned with like Manichaeism and Mithraism. What the Alexandrians have to offer under the name of gnosis is of course very different from the systems of a Basilides or a Valentinus. But the Christian gnosis of Clement or Origen unequivocally explains itself as an attempt to satisfy the gnostic appetites of their contemporaries in a legitimate fashion. To the Oriental gnosis and its crude symbolism they oppose their own gnosis, which is largely derived from Greek philosophy. From Plotinus we know that the pagan Neoplatonists, too, strongly opposed the gnostic tendencies of their time.[18] Both pagan and

Christian Platonists felt that they represented the more "scientific" approach to the problem, because their basis was the Greek intellectual tradition. This tradition offered them the distinction of an esoteric and an exoteric kind of knowledge that corresponded to the contrast of truth (*aletheia*) and mere appearance (*doxa*). Such a distinction was made by more than one philosophical system of their time. It was even interpreted back into the older systems, like those of Plato and Aristotle, or led to mystifications such as an alleged esoteric Pythagoreanism, for which a fictitious literature was created that they projected back to the time of Pythagoras himself and his initiated pupils. Christian theology easily lent itself to a similar interpretation, and the idea of the Christian religion as a mystery, which soon was generally adopted and became predominant in Christian literature and worship, favored this development.

The sharp polemic of Clement against the pagan mystery religions in his *Protrepticus* is more easily explained when we consider that from the fourth century B.C. on, the form of Greek religion that appealed most to the people of higher education was not the religion of the Olympic gods but that of the mysteries, which gave the individual a more personal relationship to the godhead. Wherever philosophers compared their teachings to religious wisdom, they referred to the mysteries as the higher form of religion that had a

message for mankind.[19] This comparison was very old;
it is found even among other seekers after the hidden
truth, in the Hippocratic writings, for instance, where
the doctor who possesses true medical knowledge is
likened to one initiated in the holy mysteries, in order
to distinguish him from the charlatan and the ignorant
layman.[20] This is an ever-increasing trend in Greek
philosophy as time goes on; it is of course most natural
in the language of philosophical theology. In the language of Clement and Origen the word mystery is
used very frequently, and what had first been meant
as a mere metaphor now became a real thing. The
gnosis that Christian theology pretended to offer was
for its followers the only true mystery in the world
that would triumph over the many pseudo-mysteries
of the pagan religion.[21] The claim of Christianity to
be a message for all men seems to contradict such a
distinction of the faithful who have only their simple
faith and those who are in possession of a higher and
secret gnosis; but this tendency seems to have been
almost irresistible in Clement's time and particularly
at Alexandria, the meeting-ground of so many mystery
cults. A heretical group like the Carpocratians, which
developed there in Clement's time, boasted of the possession of a secret version of the Gospel of Mark that
contained their doctrine but was allegedly withheld
by the church and reserved for the few who were
permitted to read it. Clement in a letter rediscovered

only recently explains that such a secret version of a more complete version of Mark does indeed exist, but that the version circulated by the heretic sect of the Carpocratians is a bad mixture of the genuine secret Gospel of Mark and the favorite errors of the sect that the Carpocratians had interpolated into it.[22] The temptation to produce such secret versions must have been great at a time that assumed the existence of esoteric sources for almost every philosophic sect. Even orthodox Christianity needed its hierophantic interpretation, which could pass as its special brand of gnosis — the true gnosis, as opposed to the "pseudonymous gnosis" of "those outside" (*hoi exo*).

A word has to be said here about the literary form in which the new intellectual life in the Christian school of Alexandria appears. Origen's thought represents a more advanced stage of this development, whereas Clement, his predecessor, is still close to the Apologists and can be called the last and most important of that group. Accordingly, Origen's and Clement's writing differ greatly in form. Origen is the scholarly mind. He employs, for the first time in Christian literature, the traditional forms of Greek scholarship, such as critical edition, commentary, scholion, scientific treatise, dialogue, to display his immense learning and put it at the disposal of future generations. He keeps this part of his writing strictly separate from his sermons, which are of an edifying character.[23] The tone of his scientific books is sober and rational, and St. Jerome in the preface to his commentary on Isaiah, avowedly written to make Origen's learned theology known to the Latin-speaking Western world, expresses some doubt as to the effect it will have on the Western Church, where people admire and desire a display of declamatory eloquence and nothing else.[24] That characterizes Origen very well as a late heir of the Greek scientific spirit, the spirit of profound research and dedication to a life of *theoria*. It is reflected even in his manner of writing, which, although clear and well ordered, is free from the stylistic classicism of his age and stresses content rather than form. The great works *De principiis* and *Contra Celsum* reveal him as a master of philosophical discussion in the manner of contemporary Greek literature, whereas in his commentaries he uses the methods and writes in the terms of the textual criticism and exegetic literature developed by the Alexandrian school of philology that had flourished centuries before his time. He reflects the voluminous learning of that school also in the enormous dimensions of his scholarly production, which presupposes an ascetic type of personality. Even so, it would be hard to understand his achievement without remembering that he dictated all his works to a staff of secretaries who took notes in turn all day long.

Clement is a writer of different caliber. In his *Protrepticus* he takes over a literary form that Greek philosophers since the times of Socrates and Aristotle had often used to invite and exhort people to adopt their way of life. Philosophy was commended in the protreptic *logos* as the road to happiness and as the knowledge of the aim of man's life that was necessary to acquire the true good.[25] This form of speech had often changed in accordance with the type of philosophy it represented, and it was not as stereotyped as scholars have sometimes imagined. I have shown this in the *Protrepticus* of Aristotle,[26] and Clement's praise of Christianity is indeed very different from such pagan models. It is to a large extent polemical against Greek religion and philosophy, but the imitation of the philosophical type of this literary genus is nevertheless obvious. Clement's *Stromata* also had a Greek model. His language is of a much more pretentious and elaborate character than Origen's. It too is an imitation of the literary fashion of the second Sophistic movement that started in the second century. It is highly declamatory and does not disdain to employ the means and effects of contemporary rhetorical style.[27] Even before Clement, the development of Christian literature, especially homiletic literature, had gone a long way to meet the requirements of the modern Asianic eloquence dominant in secular literature. The discovery of a sermon by the bishop Melito of Sardis (middle of the second century) preserved on papyrus [28] was a great surprise when compared with the so-called Second Letter of Clement of Rome, which is in reality the oldest Christian sermon we have in postapostolic literature. From the artless simplicity of that document it is a far remove to the overblown mannerism of Melito's Easter sermon, with its endless cascades of anaphoras and the tragic dramatization of its subject, the slaying of the first-born sons of the Egyptians by the angel of Jahwe. Clement of Alexandria does not sermonize, he argues. But his prose is often close to poetry, and its rhythm, which imitates musical measures, is not always pleasant to the modern ear.

In his *Paedagogus* Clement aims at Greek culture, the Hellenic paideia. In this book he portrays Christ in his role as the divine educator who transcends anything of this kind that has appeared before in human history. Up to this point we have compared these Christian thinkers with their Greek cultural forebears as far as their philosophy and their literary form goes; we now witness their attempt to face the cultural idea of the Greeks as a whole.[29] They try to see Christianity in the light of the supreme concept of what the Greeks had contributed to the higher life of the human race. They do not deny the value of that tradition, but they claim that their faith fulfills this paideutic mission of mankind to a higher degree than had been achieved before. Considering the importance of this overarching idea of paideia for the evolution of a unified culture in the Greek intellectual world, this step in the discussion between Christianity and the Hellenistic tradition marks the beginning of a decisive development in the aspiration of the Christians toward the goal of a Christian civilization, as will soon become clear. Clement vacillates between sharp polemical utterances that flatly reject the religious value of the older pagan culture and an occasional fairer cultural appreciation of its historical merits. When he is confronted with a phenomenon hard for him to accept yet impossible to deny, such as the spiritual rank of Plato's philosophy, he must either assume that it is all derived from Moses and that Plato is a *Moyses attikizon,* or admit that it is the Old Testament of the pagan world, whatever its historical relation to the Hebrew tradition.[30] As a true Christian, Clement cannot believe that the Greek philosophers, if they were able to recognize a part of the truth, could have achieved it by mere chance and without divine dispensation.[31] From this point of departure his theological thought advances toward a new view of divine providence. Following the Greek historians of philosophy, Clement distinguishes a philosophy of the barbarians and one of the Greeks:[32] this makes it easier for him to see a plan in the evolution of the human mind. The two supplement each other, and thus Clement recognizes philosophy, though it is not perfect, as the propaideia of the perfect gnostic.[33] The true paideia is the Christian religion itself, but Christianity in its theological form, as conceived in Clement's own system of Christian gnosis, for it is obvious that the interpretation of Christianity as gnosis per se implies that it is the divine paideia.

We observe how in various passages of his works Clement recurs to the problem and opens a window through which we see the world in this new perspective. It is obvious that the question, which is essential to him, must lead further and have consequences for the way in which Christianity understands itself. We find this confirmed when we read Origen, who takes up his ideas and develops them with stronger consistency and in greater detail. Indeed, they permeate his entire thought. If we ask where we can grasp the intrinsic unity of Origen's diffused and vast theological thought, we see that it is to be found not in his adherence to any single philosophical system such as Platonism or Stoicism or in an eclectic mixture of these but in the basic view of history emerging from the constellation of an age that saw classical Greek culture and the Christian church undergo a process of mutual adaptation. The merging of the Christian religion with the Greek intellectual heritage made people realize that both traditions had much in common when they were viewed from the higher vantage point of the Greek idea of paideia or education, which offered a unique general denominator for both. We have found the idea of such a merger anticipated as early as Paul's speech in Athens in Acts, a book of broad historical vision, but it now comes to its full fruition. Origen's thought leads to a real philosophy of history, a thing that never grew on the soil of classical Greece because the Greeks of that period were concerned only with themselves and not with other civilizations. In Herodotus they came nearest to such a philosophy, or rather theology, of history, but on the whole they were more interested in the typical evolution of man from the primitive stage to higher culture than in speculation about the historical architecture of the human mind and its development. Their attempts at demonstrating cultural evolution either in terms of Democritean causality or of Aristotelian teleology could not satisfy a Christian thinker. His basically different concept of cosmology (cosmogony as creation) necessitated a philosophy of the mind and of human culture that looked for a plan in the world of history comparable to the divine planning of the physical world. Christian historical thought had to take account of the fact of the ever-increasing coordination and cooperation of the various human races under the Christian faith. The Greek idea of the future unity of mankind under Greek paideia, as it appears in Isocrates [34] as early as the fourth century B.C., had become a reality after Alexander's conquest of the East. Using this international culture as its basis, Christianity now became the new paideia that had as its source the divine Logos itself, the Word that had created the world. Both Greeks and barbarians were its instruments.

Origen's philosophical passion is not merely an academic affair. We must see it against the background of the strong Manichaean and gnostic currents of the Eastern religious syncretism of Origen's time. We must contrast it with the deep pessimism that weighed down the minds of countless thinking men who saw the forces of evil prevail over the good everywhere in the world. Against these tides of discouragement Plato stood like a rock with his conviction that the seed of the good is to be found in everything and in the nature of being itself.[35] Only that which he calls the *agathoid* element in all things really "is." On that ground man could build a Christian world and justify the Creator's approval of his own work when he found it good. But how can we reconcile this claim with another equally strong Jewish and Christian conviction, namely, the sinfulness of human nature? It was even harder to accept for those who believed that Christ had come to redeem the world but who now had to admit that men went on sinning even after their salvation. If God was almighty, why did He not prevent sin by creating man perfect and guiltless? Why was it necessary for God to descend from heaven and assume human form in order to make good His failure to exclude man's transgression from the start? Philosophy had taught that man's dignity was his free will, the existence of which was of course denied by those who believed that evil was an independent, self-propagating force in the world and was deeply rooted in human nature. The Christians themselves assumed that man's will was no longer as free as it had been when he came perfect from the hands of the Creator. But they could not admit, on the other hand, that it was impossible for him to choose between good and evil and decide in favor of the good, even after the purity of his nature had been obscured by the fall of Adam.

Origen conceived man as a free moral agent, and therefore could not feel that God's creation would be more perfect if He had deprived man of this essential quality, the capacity for freely choosing the good for its own sake. Thus his Platonic and Stoic belief became the point of departure for his entire construction of man's history. Everything depends on man's ability to know what is the good and to distinguish it from the bad, or, to put it in Platonic terms, everything depends on man's ability to tell the real good from the mere appearance of good, the true from the false, being from non-being. Starting from there, philosophy for Plato had become paideia, the education of man. And that was how Origen understood Christianity. It was the greatest educational power in history and was in essential agreement with Plato and philosophy. So Plato and philosophy became for Origen the most powerful allies of Christianity in its present fight.

The next question was how this scheme of education and the gradual liberation of the human will was related to Christ. Christ to Origen was the great teacher, and in this respect his view of Christianity as the paideia of mankind permitted him to stay close to the Scriptures and to the picture the gospels give of Jesus. But Jesus is not a self-appointed human teacher; in him is embodied the divine Logos. This is the great difference of Christianity from all mere human philosophy, that it represents the coming of the Logos to man not only as a human effort but as proceeding from a divine initiative. But had not Plato, in his last great work, the *Laws*, taught that the Logos is the golden link through which the Lawgiver and Teacher and his work are connected with the divine Nous? [36] Had he not placed man in a universe that in its perfect order and harmony was an eternal model for the life of man? The cosmos of Plato's *Timaeus* made the education of man possible, for it requires for its realization a cosmic and not a chaotic world. In his *Laws* we find a statement that relates all that is said in that work about the right paideia to God as its ultimate source. God is the pedagogue of the universe, *ho theos paidagogei ton kosmon.*[37] Protagoras the sophist had once declared that man is the measure of all things, but that made all education relative. Plato reverses this famous sentence of Protagoras and emends it to, God is the measure of all things.[38] Christ

66

is for Origen the educator who transfers these sublime ideas to reality. But for him the salvation that comes through Christ is not a single historical event. Unique in its importance as it is, it had been preceded by many steps of a similar nature, beginning with Creation itself, which made man into an image of God; and after the fall of Adam there was the long line of the prophets of Israel and the great philosophers of Greece and the wise lawgivers through whom God had "spoken," if we may use such an anthropomorphic expression. The Stoics had introduced the concept of *pronoia*, a divine providence that takes care of the world and of mankind. They saw the evidence of it in the entire nature of the cosmos. Its eternal laws reveal the divine Logos that penetrates all being. Origen finds the evidence of this Logos and of Providence in the history of humanity, and builds up a picture of history that comprises and welds together the facts both of biblical history and of the history of the Greek mind. Paideia is thus the gradual fulfillment of the divine providence.[39]

V I

IT is not possible in the limited space at my disposal to trace the theological consequences of this conception of Christianity. We must content ourselves with the recognition of the important historical fact that Origen's theology is based on the Greek idea of paideia in its highest philosophical form.[1] Thus it becomes for him the key to the problem of the true relationship of the Christian religion and Greek culture. It is the greatest attempt so far made to incorporate culture in the Greek sense of the word in Christianity and to interpret Christianity and its historical mission in Greek philosophical terms. If we really want to understand Origen, it will not help much to measure him by the single dogmatic issues (Trinity, Incarnation, and so forth) of the following centuries and to ask how far he has anticipated each of them or to observe how inarticulate or wrong he appears with regard to some of them. Nor is it sufficient to apply to him the good old-fashioned methods of nineteenth century *Quellenanalyse* and ask who are the philosophical authors who have influenced him most. Rather, we have to face the structure of his thought as a whole and to ask what is the function that certain leading ideas have in it. His basic manner of presentation is that of the exegete; he moves with his texts and is led along by what they say. But there are clearly certain motifs that occur again and again and determine the nature of the questions he raises. Among them the paideia-concept of the Greeks is of fundamental importance. This is due not only to Origen's personal inclinations but to the central position it had occupied in Greek thought for centuries. We cannot therefore explain its importance for him by taking him as an isolated phenomenon. The true meaning of the thing will appear only against the background of the entire history of the Hellenic paideia, the effects of which extend far beyond the limits of the national culture of classical Hellas. By taking up this central idea and giving it its own interpretation, the Christian religion proved capable of giving the world more than just another religious sect. It ceased merely to defend itself, and offered its own positive philosophy as a basis for a reconciliation of the old and the new world. Origen died a martyr. The times were not yet ripe for his ideas.

I have dwelt at length on the Alexandrian school and the origin of Christian theology, but this is indeed the most important phase in the relationship of Christianity and Greek culture. It would be vain to strive for completeness, yet I cannot conclude my treatment of this problem without casting a last glimpse at the great fathers of the church in the fourth century, after

Christianity had been officially admitted to the Roman Empire by Constantine. It was only at the end of the fourth century, under Theodosius, that Christianity became the public religion of the Roman state; however, its situation changed radically as soon as the persecutions had come to an end. Christianity now occupied a powerful position in the Empire. But it could not fulfill the unifying and consolidating function for which it had been chosen by the ruler of the state if it did not (1) overcome the conflict within its own ranks as to what was to be regarded as the authentic form of the Christian faith, and whether Christ, after whom it was named, was really its god or was not a god at all, as the followers of Arius insisted; and (2) prove itself capable of attracting the large and important percentage of the pagan population still opposed to it.

This percentage of the people derived from the highest strata of society; but whereas at certain times and places in the history of the church they could be regarded as a *quantité négligeable*, they had a much greater influence in a civilization that had higher education as its social foundation. For a large part of this class of people, the resistance to Christianity was not in the first place an internal religious problem or a positive faith, but a cultural issue. The tradition of their classical education had become for them a religion and had considerable power, since many of them were men in the highest positions in state and society. So they were a factor to be reckoned with. In former centuries, whenever an old religious tradition such as the belief in the gods of the Athenian city-state or the Roman republic had been in danger in times of political decline, the most cultured element of human society had made the maintenance of the old religion an article of faith for educated persons, as Isocrates had done in Athens or as Varro had done in Rome in his learned work *Antiquitates rerum humanarum et divinarum.*[2] They defended the faith of their fathers as a part of their social and political heritage, and they dreaded new forms of religious cult as providing a transition to new kinds of superstition. While in the East this resistance came from the emperor Julian himself, one generation after Constantine had officially bowed to Christianity, in contemporary Rome (or just a little later) we find an exact parallel: the famous fight of the senator Symmachus, leader of the conservative opposition, and his aristocratic followers against the removal of the altar of the goddess Victoria from the curia, the meeting-place of the Roman senate in the forum. In both cases, that of Julian's systematic persecution of Christianity and that of the desperate fight of Symmachus and his party, it is quite clear that the leading minds of the pagan opposition are representatives of the highest cultural tradition. Their point of departure is their culture, the paideia that for cen-

71

turies had been the unifying cultural ideology of the Roman Empire and the civilization for which it stood.

When under Julian this anti-Christian policy was adopted by the ruler of the state, who returned to "Hellenism" in its total form, that slogan came to mean a cultural and political classicism, including the old religious cults of the pagan gods; in other words, the Greek paideia became a religion and an article of faith.[3] Religion was an object of political and educational pagan restoration. In this form the church could only be hostile to it. The unintellectual stratum of the Christian population probably were anyhow. But this is the point where the Christians of higher cultural ambition and greater political foresight could not follow such mass instincts; rather, they rose to the occasion under a wise leadership, and instead of rejecting this culture out of hand they made a supreme effort to distinguish, in the new and artificially galvanized "Hellenism," the element that was dead before it was born from the lasting and vital force that they needed. They felt that the entire apparatus of pagan oracles and mystery cults and astrological superstition ought not be taken too seriously. But, on the other hand, if Christianity proved unable to take over cultural and intellectual leadership, even its external political victory, of which they felt certain in the long run, would be illusory. It was not enough to coin slogans and to proclaim Christ the new pedagogue of humanity, as

Clement of Alexandria had done, and Christianity as the only true paideia. Christians had to show the formative power of their spirit in works of superior intellectual and artistic caliber and to carry the contemporary mind along in their enthusiasm. That new enthusiasm might become the creative new force that was needed, but it would never achieve its goal without passing through the severest training of hand and mind, just as the ancient Greeks had had to learn the hard way. They had to start from the elements and then build man up systematically. What they needed was the kind of school that would teach them that. In a word, they had to build up a Christian paideia.

When we compare a great theologian of the time of the Council of Nicaea (325) with the theological leaders of the generation of the Cappadocian fathers in the second half of the fourth century, it is obvious that this is the way in which they are going. There is of course a strict continuity among them so far as their constructive work within the church and its great dogmatic controversies are concerned. What Athanasius achieved as a ruler of the church and as a fighter and sufferer for his cause is carried on in the more systematic polemic of the next generation and in its vast theological speculation about Trinity and Incarnation. But there is a new emphasis by the men of that generation on the cultural problem. The Cappadocians, Basil and the two Gregories, do not proclaim programs for

73

the development of the Christian religion in their time, but they reveal their ideas at every step in their work. They are great theologians, but they are more than that. Even in their high appreciation of Origen, to whom they often refer, they show that they, like him, think of theology as a great science based on supreme scholarship and as a philosophical pursuit of the mind. And this science is part of the entire civilization that is theirs and in which they feel at home.

That was not possible without profound thought about the relationship of Christianity and the Greek heritage. Origen and Clement had started this line of thought on a high level, but now much more was needed. Origen had given the Christian religion its own theology in the style of the Greek philosophical tradition, but what the Cappadocians had in mind was a whole Christian civilization. They brought to that task a broad culture that is manifest everywhere in their writings. Notwithstanding their religious convictions, which are opposed to the revival of the classical Greek religion attempted by powerful forces in the state at their time,[4] they do not conceal their high esteem for the cultural heritage of ancient Greece. This is the sharp line of demarcation that they draw between Greek religion and Greek culture. Thus they came to revive the positive and productive relation of Christianity and Hellenism that we found in Origen, but in a new form and on a different level. It is not say-

74

ing too much if in their case we speak of a kind of Christian neoclassicism that is of more than merely formal character. Christianity through them now emerges as the heir to everything in the Greek tradition that seemed worthy of survival. It thereby not only fortifies itself and its position in the civilized world, but preserves and revives a cultural heritage that to a large extent, especially in the rhetorical schools of that age, had become an empty and artificial variation of a formalized classical pattern. Much has been said about the various renaissances that classical culture, both Greek and Roman, has experienced in Eastern and Western history. But little attention has been paid to the fact that we have in the fourth century A.D., the age of the great fathers of the church, a true renaissance that has given Greco-Roman literature some of its greatest personalities, figures who have exercised a lasting influence on the history and culture of later centuries down to the present day. It is characteristic of the differences between the Greek and the Roman spirits that the Latin West had its Augustine, while the Greek East through the Cappadocian fathers produced a new culture.

Of the three Cappadocians, Basil of Caesarea and Gregory of Nazianzus received a full classical education. Basil's family were city people and belonged to the propertied class of Asia Minor. Cappadocia did not have an important place in the cultural history of the country. The people were mostly horse-breeders and horse-traders, and the few major cities were stamped with the typical features of provincial life. Gregory Nazianzen was the son of a rich citizen who had been elected bishop not long after his conversion to Christianity. Gregory went to the municipal school at Nazianzus, where rhetoric was taught by imitation of classical models, so he became familiar early in life with the great authors of Greek literature. It was the same with Basil, who came from an influential and cultured Christian family in Caesarea, the capital of Cappadocia. Both were later sent to the center of higher learning, the university of Athens. It is the typical story, as we know it from the letters of Synesius, bishop of Cyrene, who himself had studied at Alexandria and whose teacher was the famous Hypatia. Writing to his brother about a sea voyage he was planning to Athens, and having asked him to forward his mail to the Piraeus, Synesius says that he hopes to find in Athens an escape from the unbearable people who come back from Athens and flood the cities of North Africa.[5] "They differ in no wise from us ordinary mortals. They do not understand Aristotle and Plato better than we, but nevertheless they go about among us like demigods among mules, because they have seen the Academy, the Lyceum, and the Stoa Poecile where Zeno gave his lectures in philosophy. However, the proconsul has taken away all the pictures from the

Poecile (which now no longer deserves its name) and has thus humiliated these men's pretensions to learning." Although this may have occurred often enough, things were different in the case of Basil and Gregory Nazianzen. Gregory of Nazianzus has told the moving story of his studies at Alexandria and Athens in his poetic autobiography, in which his friendship with Basil plays a great role.[6] They went through the regular curriculum, which included the liberal arts, rhetoric, and philosophy, all based on an extensive reading of the ancients. As Christians they stood somewhat apart socially from the other students, but that made them all the more serious about their friendship and their studies. The provincial mind had a greater receptivity than that of the normal student, and Basil's and Gregory's writings bear witness to the amazing breadth of their interests, which extended to the sciences and medicine. All this knowledge was of importance for the church later when they were the spiritual leaders of their age. They never taught these subjects, but they enlarged their intellectual horizon and raised the level of their minds. Whereas Origen's tremendous knowledge was buried in his voluminous commentaries, the Cappadocians communicated theirs to the whole Christian world, especially through the rhetorical art of their homilies.

Rhetoric and philosophy had competed from the fourth century B.C. for first place in the field of cul-

rhetoric & philosophy

ture and education. It was imperative for Christianity to put both at its service. This is what actually happened; by the end of the fourth century A.D. Christian rhetoric and philosophy dominated the scene. For our purpose it may be best, instead of generalizing, to illustrate this enormous change by the example of one man, Gregory Nazianzen, who of course is not typical in this regard but who is an outstanding representative of the cultural aspirations of the Christians. His homilies are full of classical allusions; he has a full command of Homer, Hesiod, the tragic poets, Pindar, Aristophanes, the Attic orators, the Alexandrian modernists, but also of Plutarch and Lucian and the writers of the Second Sophistic movement, who are the direct models of his style. In this respect he easily surpasses Basil and Gregory of Nyssa. He quotes or alludes to Plato many times, obviously from personal acquaintance with many of his dialogues; but his mind is not philosophical, like that of Gregory of Nyssa, who is a thinker in his own right but less brilliant in his literary form than his friend and namesake. The latter shows an aesthetic sensitivity that often has something feminine and overrefined, almost morbid, about it. He is the master of pointed, epigrammatic, and theatrical eloquence; he is carried away by emotion and passion in his speeches, though he does not have the exuberant rhetorical power of a Chrysostom. The same man is more simple and natural in his

letters, but there too his style is studied. In his letter
to Nicobulus he treats us to a discussion of the rhetorical theory of letter-writing, [7] and there is no doubt that
his rich epistolographic production was an essential
part of his literary ambition, meant, like that of a
Pliny, more for posterity than for the addressee. He
imitates the example of the personal and conversa-
tional tone of Aristotle's letters, which were still in existence at his time. Both in this display of the personal
and in the emotionality of his oratory he certainly was
the right interpreter of the psyche of his time. His
form is not original in its use of rhetorical devices, but
they serve him as a sort of symphonic instrumentation
for the display of a great new subject-matter — the
problems of Christian life and thought. The incon-
gruity of this form with our present understanding of
the Christian soul should not make us imperceptive to
what this fusion meant for Gregory's contemporaries
and to its effect on their taste and feelings. And how
enthusiastically was the Byzantine mind of the Middle Ages to respond to this hierophantic eloquence
and mentality! [8] We seem to be more ready to accept
it in his speeches than in his somewhat stilted poetry,
where the classical meter heightens the impression
of artificiality. But there develops about this time a
rich poetic productivity among the Christians, both
heretic and orthodox. I need mention only Apollinaris
of Laodicea and Synesius of Cyrene. It was the ambi-

79

tion of these men to create a real Christian literature, able to offer worthwhile products in every literary genre. In the autobiographic poem of Gregory Nazianzen, the paramount Christian interest in the inner life of a great religious individual and the interest of that lonely soul in its own spiritual growth and progress have found expression, and enriched classical literature by a new genre; it is epoch-making in the history of the literary self-manifestation of human personality, though to a lesser degree than St. Augustine's *Confessions.*[9] How much does Gregory Nazianzen gain when we compare him with the stereotyped autobiography of his famous pagan contemporary Libanius, in which the author does nothing but praise himself and his virtues throughout. I shall not go into philosophy here; but in the intellectual history of the church, philosophy on the whole was one of the basic factors of its growth, the neglect of which fact is one of the main weaknesses of recent works such as that of Lietzmann, not to speak of Cochrane.[10]

In the field of philosophy something parallel to the rhetorical and poetic culture of a Gregory Nazianzen emerged in Basil's and Gregory of Nyssa's writings, though of course Gregory Nazianzen must be given his full credit in the philosophical field too. Their free use of Greek tradition was much criticized by their contemporaries, and it is interesting to see how the Cappadocians defend their own attitude. As Moses not only

80

learned but used the wisdom of the Egyptians in which he had been initiated, so Gregory of Nyssa advocates a liberal practice in this respect, with express reference to the example set by Basil.[11] We cannot here omit consideration of Basil's famous oration on the study of Greek literature and poetry and its value for the education of Christian youth.[12] This document was the charter of all Christian higher education for centuries to come. In it the moral and religious content of ancient poetry is rejected, but its form is praised. This distinction has kept its validity for all later Christian humanism, and it well illustrates the practices of Christian writers of Basil's age. In their words they keep attacking Hellenism for its weaknesses, but in their own imitation of Greek culture they show how this polemical judgment must be modified. Their philosophy in particular shows that their admiration for things Greek goes far beyond mere forms. How should we otherwise explain the criticism of those Christians who complained that a Gregory of Nyssa was interpolating a foreign philosophy into the Bible? That they did say this we have learned just recently from the rediscovered full version of one of his later works, and I think the *Vita Moysis* was written chiefly as an answer to this accusation.[13]

On the other hand, we find no blind and uncritical enthusiasm for everything Greek in a man who could say, like Gregory of Nyssa, "Nothing is more characteristic of the Greeks [and here he must mean primarily the Christian Greeks] than their belief that the strength of Christianity lies in the dogma." [14] What an amazing distance this represents, not so much from Greek philosophical intellectualism in general but from Greek Christians, in so far as they are typical Greeks, that is, intellectualists. With this intellectualistic approach to religion he contrasts the emphasis on the "venerable customs," which apparently means the liturgical part of Christian worship with its symbolism, and the "holy mysteries" of the faith. [15] He makes this statement in the middle of a highly philosophical inquiry about the rationalistic interpretation of Christianity by the leading Arian theologian of his generation, the former bishop Eunomius of Cyzicus. Gregory stands in the Greek classical tradition, but at the same time he stands above it and is able to look at it as something foreign. This is not because he is a Christian, apparently, since he finds such intellectualism especially objectionable in Christians given too much to dogmatic hair-splitting. Perhaps there was in his nature a stronger emotional element than in these more formalistic minds, [16] and one is tempted to think of the centuries of enthusiastic religious cults that had sprung from the soil of Asia Minor, particularly the Pontus, Phrygia, and Cappadocia, from the Magna Mater of Pessinus to the Hypsistarians of Gregory's own day. When Gregory went to Jerusalem in order to worship at the holy places he remarked bitterly that he had not found a deeper religious zeal there, but much corruption, and certainly nothing that could compare with the profound religious ardor of "our Cappadocian people."[17] Perhaps underneath his polished Hellenistic culture, which had come from Athens through his brother and teacher Basil and through the schools,[18] there was a strong element of an older and more "barbarous" Cappadocian nature, and large reserves of its unspent human and emotional energy. Perhaps that mixture was one of the things that helped to fill the sclerotic arteries of the Hellenistic tradition with fresh blood. But what made him conscious of such differences was his Greek intellect.

Besides the ever-increasing influence of Greek literary and artistic form, we have traced the reception of the Greek ideal of paideia as such by the Christian writers of the third and fourth centuries. In Origen it served as the ideological framework for the systematic development of a Christian theology in which the merging of Christian religion and Greek philosophical thought reached its climax. In Gregory Nazianzen the revival of the old Greek literary forms through the infusion of the Christian spirit results in the creation of a Christian literature able to compete with the best products of contemporary pagan writing and even to surpass them in vitality and power of expression. Basil insists on the direct reception into the Christian schools, which were still *in statu nascendi,* of ancient Greek poetry as a way of higher education.[19] When we come to Gregory of Nyssa, we see him take a new approach to the problem. He himself is practically a classicist in his own writing. It is due to his activity as a teacher of rhetoric in his early years that he pays so much attention to matters of literary form, not only in his own compositions but also in his literary criticism of other writers, like his opponent the Arian Eunomius, whose style and prose rhythm Gregory censures on more than one occasion.[20] He reminds us often in his prefaces of the literary genre that he is going to use for a work, and, like Isocrates, points out what the appropriate style or length is for a particular work, or when a mixture of two literary genres may be called for in a special case. There is always conscious planning in his choice of the various forms he uses for the different purposes of his literary productivity, be it treatise, sermon, dialogue, or letter. In his language he follows the trend of contemporary classicists like Libanius and employs the neo-Attic style introduced by the so-called Second Sophistic movement; but he modifies it by a new kind of accented prose rhythm to which every sentence is subject.[21]

In the last analysis, the spectacle of this late revirescence of one of the remotest corners of the Hellenistic world, which enabled it to inspire the rest of it with fresh creative vigor, remains a miracle. One may compare it with the religious and literary renaissance of North Africa in the Latin West from the days of Tertullian, Cyprian, Arnobius, and Apuleius to Tyconius and the Donatists, and last but not least to St. Augustine of Tagaste. These provinces had much to contribute, but they needed the instrument of the Latin and Greek mind to express themselves and to communicate with each other. For all of them the Greek tradition was the ultimate cultural link. It is wrong to ask whether they always preserved the exact shade of meaning of the classical Greek archetype. What they preserved were certain basic tendencies of the classical mind around which the ideas of their own age could crystallize. Their wrestling with the classical heritage evolves in certain historical stages, which clearly show an architectonic logic in their gradual progress. The Hellenistic element constitutes its intellectual medium and determines its dialectical rhythm, a great historical rhythm that will always remain one of the reasons for our inexhaustible interest in the subject.

VII

I SHALL illustrate with the example of Gregory of Nyssa's ideas about a Christian paideia. Gregory's philosophical mind could not content itself with the sort of paideia that he had taken over from the rhetorical schools and their tradition. At his time a teacher of rhetoric was called a sophist, and it was no doubt a necessary profession. But Plato had given him a deeper idea of what the true education of man ought to be. We find him again and again concerned with this problem in his various works. The way that he approaches it shows him to be steeped in the great Greek philosophical tradition and its cultural ideals, but it also constitutes a new start toward a Christian education and the meeting of its requirements. By this we do not mean simply the teaching of Christian doctrines but the conscious attempt to arrive at a conception of the development of the human personality that could do justice to the highest demands of Greek educational philosophy. Apparently Gregory of Nyssa, more than his great brother Basil and more than Origen himself, was able to see the nature of Greek paideia in all its aspects. He understood it as the formative process of the human personality, which the great educators of Greece had sharply distinguished from the substance that is the *sine qua non* of the educational process.

Gregory recurs time and again in his works to the concept of education that was, as it were, the a priori ideal of all Greek reflection on this problem: the concept of *morphosis*.[1] His constant repetition of this basic image, which implies the essential identity of all educational activity and the work of the creative artist, painter, and sculptor, reveals the plastic nature of his conception of Greek paideia. The Christian educational ideal must therefore be realized by a return to this philosophical insight. The metaphor of the gradual growth of the human personality and its spiritual nature implies the analogy of man's physical nature; but it is specifically different from the development of the body, and the nourishment of the soul must be apportioned differently from the material food we consume. The spiritual process called education is not spontaneous in nature but requires constant care.[2] The virtues, be they moral or intellectual, are the fruit of both a man's nature and his training; but since the Christian religion has attained new insights into the complexity of man's inner life unknown to the psychology of classical Greek philosophy, the perfection of a man's *areté* for which ancient philosophers strove seems farther removed from realization than it was in classical times. The old poet Simonides, one of the great champions of the ancient

Greek ideal of *areté*, had depicted that goddess as sitting on the highest mountain cliff, inaccessible to the great mass of ordinary mortals and reached by only the most patient and tireless strivers-upward.[3] Similarly, the Christian virtue described by Gregory appears practically unattainable to any without divine help.

It must have seemed necessary to Gregory to stress this ancient idea of divine assistance, which we find expressed so often in Greek poetry from Homer on and later in Greek philosophy. This became for him the point at which the specific Christian concept of divine grace could be introduced into the scheme of classical paideia. He conceived it as the cooperation of the divine Spirit with the effort of man himself.[4] More radical theological thinkers like St. Augustine and later Martin Luther have insisted that the initiative in this process cannot come from the human side at all but only from God, and that for this reason the *synergy* or cooperation falls to man and not to God; but Gregory's concept of virtue is closer to the Greek classical tradition in this regard. He even teaches that the assistance of the divine power increases in proportion to man's own effort.[5] This is not a mere attempt to bring the Christian idea closer to the classical concept of *areté*. The true reason lies deeper. With Plato, Gregory thinks that all human will and striving by nature aims at "the good." He calls this *eros* consubstantial and connate with human nature and its true essence.[6] From this it follows that evil is essentially ignorance, since only self-delusion can cause man, the "rational animal," as Greek philosophy had defined him, to choose that which is not good for him. This logic goes a long way with Gregory, as with Plato, whose paideia ends not in this life but in the next one. As symbol of the paideutic catharsis of the soul and its alienation from evil, Gregory accepts Plato's myth and the Christian dogma of punishment in the world to come; but he does not accept the Christian idea of an eternal punishment after death. Christian paideia is conceived by this theological thinker in metaphysical terms that project its continuation into cosmic dimensions; but it reaches its conclusion in the final restoration of the perfect status of God's original creation. Here again appears his basic belief in the essential goodness of man and of the whole world, which God in the beginning created good. It is for the same reason that Christ is for Gregory the physician, the healer. For all evil is to him essentially a privation of the good. The idea of final restoration or apocatastasis comes to Gregory, along with other elements of his Platonism, from Origen, of whom Gregory's contemporary Epiphanius, bishop of Salamis, wrote in his great work on heresies that all his errors derived from his Greek paideia.[7]

If paideia was the will of God and if Christianity

was for the Christian what philosophy was for the philosopher, according to Plato — assimilation to God — the true fulfillment of the Christian ideal of life was one continuous and lifelong effort to achieve that end and to approach perfection, in so far as that was possible for man. As the Greek philosopher's whole life was a process of paideia through philosophical ascesis, so for Gregory Christianity was not a mere set of dogmas but the perfect life based on the *theoria* or contemplation of God and on ever more perfect union with Him.[8] It is *deificatio*, and paideia is the path, the divine anabasis. Basil had been the first to organize monastic life in Asia Minor and had drawn up his rule for it. In contrast to his brother, Gregory considers it his task to give that way of life its philosophy. He does so by interpreting it as the attempt at the full realization of his ideal of Christian perfection. Not all would be able to go this way, but this idea ought to permeate the entire life of the church and of every Christian as far as possible. The parallel of this conception with the Greek idea of the philosophic life as the goal and essence of all philosophy is striking, and we could not fail to notice it even if Gregory did not keep calling Christianity the "philosophic life," especially in its more strict ascetic form.[9] We cannot go into greater detail, but his comparison of Christianity with Greek philosophical paideia is of course more minute than can be traced here.

One essential feature of Greek paideia that made it unique among all the different conceptions of human education in other nations is that it not only contemplated the process of development in the human subject but also took into account the influence of the object of learning.[10] If we regard education as a process of shaping or forming, the object of learning plays the part of the mold by which the subject is shaped. The formative mold of early Greek paideia was Homer,[11] and as time went on that role was extended to Greek poetry at large. In the end, the word paideia meant Greek literature as a whole.[12] The Greeks had no other word for it. For them it was most natural to regard that which we nowadays call literature from the viewpoint of the social function it had fulfilled throughout their history. Only relatively late were the more rational branches of education added to the Greek paideia and the system of the "liberal arts" invented,[13] among them rhetoric; finally philosophy was added. To it the arts were related as propaideia, and philosophy, as Plato had conceived it, became identical with paideia itself on its highest level.[14]

Gregory's conception of Christian paideia corresponds to this Greek scheme and is practically identical with it so far as propaideia is concerned. That is how Basil and Gregory Nazianzen had received their training at Athens, and that is how Basil later trained his younger brother Gregory of Nyssa after returning from the university. Classical Greek literature was included in this system, and so was rhetoric. But what in a Christian education corresponded to the highest level of Greek paideia, the study of philosophy? As Origen had taught his students to read all the Greek philosophers, so the Cappadocians went through a serious study of this part of the classical tradition, and Gregory of Nyssa, the most philosophical of them, no doubt thought it necessary for an educated Christian to follow that difficult path. But when he speaks of paideia he chiefly has in mind that which distinguishes its Christian form from the Greek. As the Greek paideia consisted of the entire corpus of Greek literature, so the Christian paideia is the Bible. Literature is paideia, in so far as it contains the highest norms of human life, which in it have taken on their lasting and most impressive form. It is the ideal picture of man, the great paradigm. Gregory clearly sees the analogy between this Greek concept of literature and the function of the Bible. He did not read the Bible as literature, as the modern tendency is. That would be a complete misunderstanding of his concept of literature, which was the Greek concept of literature as paideia. With it he had been brought up, and the application of this sort of reading to the Christian's relation to the Bible was for him, therefore, the most natural thing in the world. He never tires of impressing this basic idea of education on his readers. The

formation of the Christian man, his *morphosis*,[15] is
the effect of his unceasing study of the Bible. The form
is Christ. The paideia of the Christian is *imitatio
Christi*: Christ must take shape in him.[16] This appears
most clearly in the manner in which Gregory quotes
the Bible as the supreme authority. Instead of saying,
"the prophet says" or "Christ says," as would be most
natural for us, he writes innumerable times, "the
prophet Isaiah educates us" or "the apostle educates
us" (*paideuei*), implying that what the Bible teaches
must be accepted as the paideia of the Christian.[17]
This very way of expressing, not so much the philological fact that this or that is written in the Bible, but
the formative function of what is written, is indicative
of his paideutic interpretation of the authority. It is
not law but education.[18] Gregory's manner of quoting
Scripture has something to do with this basic idea. He
generally uses the verb *paideuein* in connection with
the individual biblical author to whom he refers or
with the person of Christ. This is the more remarkable
since the Scripture (*he graphe*) is for Gregory nor-
mally a unity and not a collection of different authors.
It is inspired as a whole by the Holy Spirit, and from
Him the pedagogical authority of the individual biblical writers is derived.

The Spirit itself is conceived as the divine educational power that is ever present in the world and that
has spoken through the human beings who were its

instruments. The way in which the Spirit speaks to the human race in the Scriptures is that of the wise educator who never forgets the narrow limits of his pupils' capacity. If they are unable to understand the truth by immediate approach to the divine mystery, He leads them by means of symbolic expression appropriate to the sensual and finite nature of man. The anthropomorphic language used in the Scriptures with relation to things divine serves only as a starting point for the process of a deeper understanding. Gregory here follows Origen's theory of the various levels of meaning that must be distinguished in the Bible. His exegesis leads from the direct literal sense to the historical sense of the biblical text, and from this second level it advances to the higher spiritual meaning. An insight into this methodical stratification of the process of interpretation implies the educational intention of the Holy Spirit itself.[19] Only that man is a true interpreter of the sacred text who possesses the Spirit, that is to say, only the Holy Spirit is really capable of understanding itself. Accordingly Gregory invokes the Spirit when he begins his task of explaining the meaning of the divine Word, as in his large work against the Arian Eunomius or in his later treatise on the true meaning of the ascetic life. His brother Peter likewise, when he exhorts Gregory to bring to completion his great work against the Arian heresy, which denied the divinity of Christ, encourages him by saying that the Holy Spirit will come to his assistance. These are not mere words; they meant and believed them deeply. They believed in the divine inspiration of the prophets and apostles because such inspiration was a reality that they knew from their own experience.[20]

Even the historical books of the Scriptures, so Gregory assures us more than once, have this kind of spiritual and educational meaning.[21] This is not to say that they contain only a moral *fabula docet*. Let us take for instance the book *De vita Moysis*. It consists of two parts that give a perfect example of Gregory's combination of a realistic historical interpretation with a search for the pneumatic meaning of a biblical text. The first part relates the life of Moses in accordance with the tradition of the book of Exodus, that is, as a plain sequence of historical and biographical events. In the second part of the work the author gives what he calls the spiritual interpretation of this unique life and of the great religious personality who is its hero.[22] Moses here appears as the perfect model of the saint and mystic, the prototype of what Gregory calls the philosophic or contemplative life, the man whose life was lived in unceasing communion with God, who climbed up to the highest peak of his spiritual Sinai in order to see God in the darkness of the cloud. Philo had written his *Life of Moses* and so gave Gregory his literary model. He then fills his picture of Moses with the fervent life of his own mystic spirituality. Another example is the story of David, which leads Gregory to a higher level of contemplation.[23] This higher meaning could be learned even from the Book of Kings, but since it was thought, according to tradition, that the Psalms were a work of David, they revealed the secret source of that superhuman strength which was illustrated by the historical books. Basil had postulated a Christian ethics, and his commentary on the Psalms shows clearly that he wanted to use them as such.[24] On closer inspection we see that behind this interpretation there stands Basil's own experience with Aristotle's *Nicomachean Ethics*, which he had no doubt studied carefully during his stay at the school of Athens. He then had felt the need for a Christian equivalent and thought that the Psalms came closest to it. They always remained the most read portion of the Scriptures in the Christian's daily life and ascetic practice. In Gregory of Nyssa's opinion too they are one of the most wonderful examples of the paideutic work of the Holy Spirit. But this was also the way in which the letters of St. Paul were read, and there was much truth in such an interpretation of them as the most complete representation of the Christian paideia. Paul's religion is taken as a living whole but not as a historical document of Paulinism.

The Psalms show with particular clarity the influence that Gregory's paideia-theology has exercised on his interpretation of the Bible in its details. It was in-

deed much more than a fashionable general approach
or a mere tactical attempt to find a common denominator for the Christian religion and Hellenic culture,
as might appear at first sight to a superficial reader.
Let us take as an example Gregory's book *On the In-
scriptions of the Psalms.*[25] He divides the Psalter into
five parts, each of them transcending the spiritual level
of the previous part. This he shows by a comparative
study of chosen examples from each of them. The religious experience reflected in the Psalms is described
as a way from the lower to the higher level of spiritual
knowledge and divine presence. Gregory is so con-
vinced of his theory of the wise arrangement of the
material contained in the book of Psalms that his ex-
position of their order becomes a complete representation of the life of the Christian mystic who works with
all his might for his salvation and of his ascent to the
divine source of all spiritual life. The five parts of the
Psalter correspond to the stations along this path.
Whatever modern philological interpreters may think
of this method of approach, it is evident that Gregory
finds in the biblical text the immediate verification of
his theory of the steps or "grades" of the mystical way
of *theognosia.* They coincide with the steps in the
gradual formation (*morphosis*) of the perfect Christian. What in Greek paideia had been the formation
or *morphosis* of the human personality now becomes
for the Christian the *metamorphosis* of which Paul had

spoken when he wrote to the Romans, asking them to undergo a process of radical metamorphosis through a renewal of their spirit.[26] In several of his works Gregory depicts the ascent of the soul to the highest point of its journey. He illustrates the relationship of the various Christian virtues and compares their mutual connection to the links of a chain or the steps of a ladder.[27]

It is evident from our analysis of the structure of Gregory's theology that it is permeated with the Greek idea of paideia, especially in its Platonic form. Plato derives the paideia of his *Laws* from the divine *nous*. Greek philosophical education offered a complete analogy to Christian theology as Gregory understood it. This way of using the basic categories of Greek philosophy as a framework to be filled with Christian content resembles Gregory's efforts in other fields, as, for instance, when he builds up his own Christian cosmology or system of ethics as a counterpart to the corresponding forms of the Greek philosophical tradition. He uses the Greek forms as the structural model of a fully developed culture, and by way of comparison he creates for each of them a Christian variant shaped in the classical mold but at the same time clearly differentiated from it. It could not have been done otherwise. Greek culture, of course, was the product of many centuries. The attempt to take it over in a productive way and make it the instrument of the new religion was stimulating for both the traditional culture and for the Christian mind, but the result was necessarily an improvisation. In the case of Gregory of Nyssa, who had a high sensitivity to the aesthetic as well as to the philosophical values of the Greek tradition, the problem of the mutual penetration of both forces was much more on a conscious level than it was for most other Christian writers, including his brother Basil. In this respect he more resembles their common friend Gregory Nazianzen, though he is less of a literary aesthete than the latter. He is more devoted to the mystical contemplation of the one spiritual beauty, the divine archetype of all things beautiful[28] that shines through its earthly images. He connects Plato's concept of philosophy as assimilation to God with the Christian concept of man whom God created in His image.[29] Gregory's paideia is the return of the soul to God and to man's original nature.[30] The strictest form of it is his monastic ideal of the philosophic life, the life that is entirely devoted to this aim. This idea of the unification of human life in one ultimate aim (*skopos*) he shares with Plato. Gregory's lifelong interest in the institution of the monastic life and his continuous effort to imbue it with the Holy Spirit is the strongest proof of the practical nature of his educational zeal and of the dominating position the idea of Christianity as the perfect education occupied in his theology. It was Gregory of Nyssa who transferred the ideas of Greek paideia in their Platonic form into the life of the ascetic movement that originated during his time in Asia Minor and the Near East and that soon was to display an undreamed-of power of attraction.[31] From his homeland Cappadocia and the Pontus these ideas spread to Syria and Mesopotamia, where they were later taken over by Islamic mystics, and they also spread to the Latin-speaking West.

It transcends the limits of our present task to attempt to follow that process any farther East by using the unusually abundant manuscript tradition of Gregory's writings or by tracing the dissemination of his ideas. But the question how this Christian form of the Greek paideia affected the Latin world concerns us immediately. The details of this great process are to a large extent still unexplored, but they can be pursued through the Middle Ages; and from the Renaissance the line leads straight back to the Christian humanism of the fathers of the fourth century A.D. and to their idea of man's dignity and of his reformation and rebirth through the Spirit. It is true, the secularization of medieval man is one of the most frequently stressed characteristics of the Italian civilization of the fifteenth century. But with the Greeks who emigrated after the fall of Constantinople (1453) there came to Italy the whole literary tradition of the Byzantine East, and the works of the Greek fathers were its choicest part. Their influence on the thought of the Renaissance, both in Italy and throughout Europe, is still largely an unsolved problem, but the number of manuscripts of their works in the library collections of that period surpasses by far those of the classical authors. The ideological tradition of Renaissance humanism as represented by the educational thought of Erasmus has its roots in theology. This "father of modern civilization," the "prince of humanists," was a Dutch monk, and even in his later life in the "world" he remained true to the indelible form his early monastic upbringing had impressed upon his mind. In the last analysis his Christian humanism goes back to the Greek fathers who had created it in the fourth century. But his direct authorities were in the main the Latin fathers, many of whose works he edited, along with the New Testament. St. Augustine's name comes to mind first of all in this connection. He lived only one generation after the Cappadocian fathers, with whom he shares so many characteristic features in a way that is still unexplained. Jerome and Ambrose hold a place of honor beside him.[32] When we look at the problem from this angle, it is evident that what we have been dealing with in this study is not only the last chapter in the history of the ideal of paideia in the late ancient Greek world but also the prologue to the history of its medieval Latin transformations. Historians have not paid much attention to the influence of this ancient Christian humanism, from which modern classical scholarship and humanism have only very lately emancipated themselves. But without it, how little of classical literature and culture would have survived!

Notes

Notes to Section I

1. Ernest Renan, *Souvenirs d'enfance et de jeunesse* (Paris 1959) p. 43f.

2. In theory, the influence of Greek civilization on the Christian religion has been recognized by the scholarly theological literature in many fields. In the history of dogma, Adolf von Harnack, *Lehrbuch der Dogmengeschichte* I (Freiburg-Leipzig 1894) 121–147, lists it as one of the most important factors in the shaping of the Christian religion and of its historical development. Harnack's fundamental work has in particular shown the nature of the impact of Greek philosophy on Christian doctrine. The philosophical implications of Christian doctrine and their Greek origin have more recently been studied in much greater detail by H. A. Wolfson, *The Philosophy of the Church Fathers* I (Cambridge, Mass., 1956). Even before this systematic attempt, the theological generation that followed Harnack's historical school had traced the Greek element in the biblical books themselves, particularly in the New Testament, and Hans Lietzmann's great *Handbuch zum Neuen Testament* systematically applied this point of view to the exegesis of the earliest Christian documents. E. R. Goodenough has more recently shown the Greek influence on late Judaism in the archaeological field in his *Jewish Symbols in the Greco-Roman Period* (8 vols., New York 1953–1958). The so-called general history of religion has approached foreign religious influence on early Christianity on a broader front, but it has also touched upon the influence of the Greeks. On the other hand, a direct impact of Greek philosophy on the New Testament, and in particular on St. Paul, which former schools of theological studies

105

(e.g., that of D. F. Strauss) used to assume, has not been confirmed by modern historical research. To be sure, there were many philosophical ideas in the air, but that is not the same thing as a demonstrable doctrinal influence, e.g., of Seneca on St. Paul, such as was assumed by the mid-nineteenth century Tübingen school of theology. On the whole, this kind of doctrinal influence of Greek philosophy on Christian thought belongs to later generations; see pages 64f, 86ff. On reminiscences of classical literature and literary forms, see pages 7, 57; on the knowledge of the Greek language in Jewish and Jewish-Christian environments, cf. pages 5–12.

3. This aspect has chiefly been stressed for the last half century in Christian theological research, ever since Harnack felt it necessary to raise the battle cry and try to stem the tide of comparative *Religionsgeschichte* of the type favored by R. Reitzenstein and other contemporary scholars, who seemed to be threatening to destroy the originality of the Christian religion and to obscure its real origin as a phase in the history of the Jewish mind. On this late period of Jewish religion, see the standard work of Emil Schürer, *Geschichte des jüdischen Volkes im Zeitalter Jesu Christi* (4th ed., Leipzig 1901–1909; English translation by J. Macpherson, S. Taylor, and P. Christie, New York 1891). See also R. Pfeiffer, *History of New Testament Times* (New York 1949).

4. J. G. Droysen, *Geschichte des Hellenismus* (Hamburg 1836–1843).

5. J. G. Droysen, *Briefwechsel*, ed. Rudolf Hübner (Berlin-Leipzig 1929) I, 70: "Die Geschichte der hellenistischen Jahrhunderte ist, wie mir scheint, von Philologen und Theologen und Historikern auf gleich arge Weise vernachlässigt. Und doch ist es aus dem Hellenismus, dass das Christentum seinen Ursprung und die merkwürdigsten Richtungen seiner ersten Entwicklungen genommen hat. Die wunderbare Erscheinung einer Weltbildung, einer Weltliteratur, einer gänzlichen Aufklärung, welche die Jahrhunderte nach Christi Geburt

charakterisiert, ist nicht innerhalb des Christentums noch des Römertums, sondern nur in der Geschichte des Hellenismus begreiflich." It is evident from this letter that the interest of the discoverer of the history of Hellenism was due partly to the period itself but partly, and perhaps more, to the role it played in world history as the development that made Christianity possible.

6. *Hellenismos*, which is the noun derived from the verb *hellenizo* ("to speak Greek"), originally meant the correct use of the Greek language. The concept seems to have been first employed by the teachers of rhetoric. Theophrastus, who like his master Aristotle made rhetoric a part of his teaching in the Lyceum at Athens, built up his theory of the perfect style in five parts, which he called the "virtues of diction" (*aretai*), the first and most basic of them being *Hellenismos*, i.e., a grammatically correct use of the Greek language, Greek free from barbarisms and solecisms. (Cf. J. Stroux, *De Theophrasti virtutibus dicendi*, Leipzig 1912, p. 13.) This requirement was characteristic of the time, in fourth century Greece, when foreigners of every social status had become so numerous that they exercised a deteriorating influence on the spoken idiom, even on the language of the Greeks themselves. The word *Hellenismos* thus did not originally have the meaning of adopting Greek manners or a Greek way of life that it later inevitably assumed, especially outside Hellas where Greek culture became the fashion. On another late-ancient use of the word that developed in a world already to a large extent Christianized, see page 72. It then came to mean not only the culture and language of the Greeks but also the "pagan," i.e., ancient Greek, cult and religion. In this sense it is much used by the Greek church fathers in their polemic. These various meanings of the word are not always sufficiently distinguished in the scholarly literature.

7. This was true of course most of all for the Jewish aristocracy and the educated class; Josephus, *Antiquitates Judaicae*

XX.12.264 (*Opera*, ed. Niese, IV, Berlin 1890, 269) rightly observes that the great mass of the Jewish people are less inclined than other nations to learn foreign languages, This was different for Jews living outside Palestine in a Hellenized environment, where they soon made Greek their language rather than Egyptian or other native tongues. But in Palestine too Greek was understood and was used in trade and business, even by the less educated, to a much greater extent than scholars have often assumed; cf. S. Lieberman, *Greek in Jewish Palestine* (New York 1942), and the same author's *Hellenism in Jewish Palestine* (New York 1950).

8. Acts 6.1ff. The word "Hellenists" occurs here in contradistinction to "Hebrews," but it does not mean "Greeks" (a word that is used for "gentiles" in the New Testament); it is the official term for the Greek-speaking element among the Jews, and consequently also among the early Christian community in Jerusalem at the time of the apostles. It does not mean Jews born or brought up in Jerusalem who had adopted Greek culture, but people who no longer spoke their original Aramaic at home, even if they understood it, but Greek, because they or their families had lived abroad in Hellenized cities for a long time and later had returned to their homeland. Those of them who had not become Christians had their own Hellenistic synagogues in Jerusalem, and we find a Christian Hellenist like Stephen involved in long religious discussions with them. The synagogues of the Libertinoi, the Cyrenaeans, the Alexandrians, the Cilicians, and all the synagogues of Asia Minor are mentioned (Acts 6.9) expressly. It was natural that the Christian Hellenists, even while still doing missionary work in Jerusalem before the death of Stephen, should have turned first of all to these non-Christianized Hellenists among the Jews and to their schools because of the common link of their Greek background of language and education. That they were an increasingly strong minority in the apostolic community must be concluded from the fact that they insisted on having

their own Greek-speaking representatives for the daily distribution of food and other help among their widows. They were able to obtain from the twelve apostles the important concession of the institution of the new office of deacons. Since the first deacons listed in Acts 6.5 all have Greek names, it seems clear that they were the special representatives only for the Greek-speaking members of the community, and were supposed to take over primarily the care of that part of the congregation. The apostles, in announcing that innovation, stress that it would be too much work for them to do all by themselves. If, however, the new deacons were meant to take over the care of the entire congregation, Hellenists and "Hebrews" alike, it would increase still more the importance of the Hellenists within the early Christian community, because the seven who were elected deacons were all Hellenists.

9. Only Nikolaos was not a Jew by birth, but had been a proselyte from Antioch before his conversion to the Christian faith; cf. Acts 6.5.

10. Acts 11.26.

11. There are differences in this respect between the gospels and St. Paul. In his letters the number of Old Testament quotations taken from the LXX exceeds overwhelmingly those taken from other sources. Cf. H. B. Swete, *Introduction to the Old Testament in Greek*, 2nd ed. (Cambridge 1914) p. 381ff.

12. On this problem in general, see Paul Wendland, *Die urchristlichen Literaturformen* (Tübingen 1912), Part 3 of H. Lietzmann's *Handbuch zum Neuen Testament* I.

13. Cf. H. Musurillo, *The Acts of the Pagan Martyrs* (Oxford 1954), especially p. 236f.

14. Plato, *Rep.* II.364e, speaks of a "heap of treatises" offered by the "wandering prophets" of Musaeus and Orpheus in which they taught a cathartic religion and its rituals called *teletai* (i.e., initiations). A little before this passage (364b–c) he has said that these prophets went to the doors of the rich in order to make converts to their sect among them, giving in-

struction in rituals and sacrifices through which they might obtain absolution from their old sins or those of their ancestors. The treatises contained practical advice about the various methods conducive to that purpose. See O. Kern, *Orphicorum Fragmenta* (Berlin 1922) p. 81f.

15. This is the meaning of the words of Plutarch, *Praecepta coniugalia* c. 19 (*Moralia* I, ed. Paton-Wegehaupt, Leipzig 1925, p. 288, 5–10). Cf. my *Scripta Minora* (Rome 1960) I, 136.

16. James 3.6. Cf. Hans Windisch, *Die katholischen Briefe*, 3rd ed. (Tübingen 1951; *Handbuch zum Neuen Testament*, XV) p. 23, on this passage, and Kern, *Orphicorum Fragmenta* p. 244.

17. Cf. *Scripta Minora* I, 140.

18. Hesiod, *Works and Days* 288–293.

19. Cf. *Scripta Minora* I, 140f.

20. Didache c. 1–6, in *Die apostolischen Väter*, ed. Karl Bihlmeyer (Tübingen 1924). The same extensive treatment of the "two ways" is found in the Epistle of Barnabas c. 18, *ibid.* Since certain differences in the arrangement of the material in both documents makes it impossible to derive either from the other, it seems evident that both depend on a common source. This source appears to have been a moralizing Jewish tract, and indeed the doctrine of the two ways itself has little or nothing that could be called specifically Christian. The Neo-Pythagorean *Pinax of Cebes* (cf. note 19), which contains the same moral doctrine, proves beyond reasonable doubt that ultimately it stems from a Hellenistic source that was neither Jewish nor Christian.

21. Democritus frg. 3, Diels-Kranz, *Fragmente der Vorsokratiker* II [8].132. This book has undergone later expansions, owing to its great popularity, and parts of it found their way even into the late-ancient collections of moral proverbs and apophthegms such as the florilegium of Stobaeus. It was still widely read during the age of the Roman emperors. The Shep-

herd of Hermas too is a *Volksbuch,* as its varying text-transmission has proved. Cf. *A Papyrus Codex of the Shepherd of Hermas* (Similitudes 2–9), ed. Campbell Bonner (Ann Arbor 1934) p. 23ff.

22. *Hermae Pastor,* Sim. IV.5, in *Patres Apostolici,* ed. Gebhardt-Harnack-Zahn, 4th ed. (Leipzig 1902) p. 171, 4ff.

23. Philo, e.g., *Quod deterius potiori insidiari soleat,* I.292.24.

24. The most typical example of a Socratic protreptic speech or exhortation is found in Plato's dialogue *Euthydemus;* cf. my *Aristotle* [2] (Oxford 1948) p. 62f.

25. A. D. Nock, *Conversion* (Oxford 1933), has compared the conversion of new followers and the psychological attitudes of the quasi-religious philosophical sects in Hellenistic times. On the Platonic comparison of philosophy with the turning of a man's face toward the light of true Being, see my *Paideia* II (Oxford and New York 1943) 285 and especially 295ff.

26. Later, of course, the Christian apologists borrowed from the Hellenistic philosophers on a large scale, as, for example, when they made use of the polemic of the philosophers against the gods of the Greek and Roman popular religion.

27. Acts 17.17ff. To the Jews and the proselytes of Athens Paul spoke in the synagogue, so the author tells us, but the gentiles he addressed on the Areopagus, thereby referring to a rather typical situation of the apostle's missionary activity. The talks in the synagogue are only briefly mentioned, but Paul could not have omitted them, of course; the synagogue was the normal place for his sermons. But this time the emphasis is clearly on the diatribe on the Areopagus, which pictures the new situation in which the great leader of Christianity, himself both a Hellenist and a former Jew, takes aim at Christianity's final target, the classical Greek world.

28. The most thorough analysis of the argumentation in Paul's speech in Athens and its relationship to ancient Greek tradition, especially the Stoic element of it, is given by Eduard

Norden, *Agnostos Theos* (Berlin-Leipzig 1913) p. 13ff; cf. my review of that work reprinted in my *Scripta Minora* I, 110–111. I no longer believe in Norden's brilliant thesis that the author of Acts must have used as his literary pattern a work about the pagan preacher and miracle-worker Apollonius of Tyana, which would place the origin of the Acts of the Apostles well in the second century A.D. In the New Testament, quotations from Greek poetry occur several times. Clement of Alexandria, a Christian writer whose own works are full of such echoes of the Greek poets, taken partly from the texts themselves, partly from florilegia and similar collections, was the first author who paid special attention to such literary quotations in the books of the New Testament. Being himself a man of higher education, he took a great interest in the question of the Hellenic paideia of the biblical writers. He correctly identifies (*Stromata* I.19, ed. Stählin, Leipzig 1905–1909, II, 59, 1ff) the quotation in Acts 17. 28 as taken from Aratus' astronomical work *Phaenomena*, line 5. He likewise (*Strom.* I.14, Stählin II, 37, 23ff) points out the quotation of a verse of Epimenides the Cretan's epic poem, the *Oracles* (frg. 1, Diels-Kranz, *Vorsokratiker* I [8].31) in the letter to Titus 1.12; and another Greek reminiscence in I Corinthians 15.33, taken from the most famous poet of the New Attic Comedy, Menander (*Thaïs* frg. 218, *Comicorum Atticorum Fragmenta*, ed. Kock, III, Leipzig 1888, 62) – a very appropriate quotation in a letter of Paul addressed to the most educated Greek congregation in Corinth.

29. There can be little doubt among scholars who know the traditions of ancient historical writing that Paul's speech in Athens has only typical verisimilitude, but is not a historical document. The author, who wrote it to serve as the dramatic climax of his whole book, had not only studied Greek historical works but was himself a man of true historical vision, as is obvious from the sovereign manner in which he handles his material and skillfully balances its parts. Cf. A. v. Harnack, "Ist die Rede des Paulus in Athen ein ursprünglicher Bestand-

teil der Apostelgeschichte?" in *Texte und Untersuchungen,* 3rd Series, IX, No. 1 (Leipzig 1913). On the author of Acts as a historian, see Eduard Meyer, *Ursprung und Anfänge des Christentums* (Stuttgart 1921–1923) III, 3 and 23.

30. Acta Philippi c. 8 (3). Cf. *Acta Apostolorum Apocrypha,* ed. Lipsius-Bonnet, II, Part 2 (Leipzig 1903) p. 5, 2.

Notes to Section II

1. Officially, at that time, the church in Rome and the church in Corinth were coordinated churches, since "the church" was a unity only in so far as the idea was concerned; the unity, however, is stressed more and more as time goes on, as we observe even in the New Testament itself, e.g., in the Epistle to the Ephesians, which in this respect foreshadows the actual development of the universal church in the following centuries.

2. Clement, I Epist. ad Corinth. c. 3f. On the technical use of examples as a means of persuasion in Greek rhetoric, cf. note 3. *Stasis* (discord, party strife) is one of the most discussed problems in Greek political thought.

3. Clement preaches concord, as he warns of discord and *stasis,* by giving many examples. In the course of this argument the emphasis on concord gradually shifts to obedience, and even to faith. But the rhetorical treatment of the subject is the same. We cannot here enter into a detailed history of the political idea of *homonoia* (concord) in Greek literature (cf. Harald Fuchs, "Augustin und der antike Friedensgedanke," in *Neue philologische Untersuchungen,* ed. W. Jaeger, III, Berlin 1926, 109ff) from Solon's elegy *Eunomia* or Aeschylus' *Eumenides* and the sophist Antiphon's prose book on this subject through the Greek orators and political thinkers down to the declamations of the rhetorical schools of Clement's time. It is to the latter that the Christian bishop's technique

and treatment of this theme must be traced, and not to the older sources mentioned above. From the rhetorical schools of his own day is derived the extensive use that Clement makes of proof by accumulated examples. In the Scriptures this method of demonstration is not very common yet, but where we observe it, as for example in the Epistle to the Hebrews, it is due to the same influence of contemporary rhetorical art. Some of Clement's examples are taken from this book, as it seems, but the method as such both writers took from the current practice and handbooks of rhetorical *techné*.

From them Clement borrowed among other things the distinction of examples from the past and examples taken from more recent historical experience (cf. 5.1), which the rhetoricians had so often observed in the classical Greek orators such as Demosthenes and Isocrates. A negative *topos* like "Disunity and strife have often destroyed powerful states and great nations," which Clement uses in I Epist. ad Corinth. 6.4, also goes back to that source. It is the rhetorical figure of *amplificatio* by which the speaker shows that the thing of which he is speaking has often been the cause of great benefits (or great evils). Even poetry was invaded by such rhetorical devices; for example, when Catullus translates (carm. 51) some stanzas of Sappho's famous poem, no doubt after discovering it in some handbook of rhetoric (it is exactly such a rhetorical treatise that has preserved it to us), he adds a moral as a last stanza and admonishes his better self not to indulge too much in "otium," which "has already ruined powerful kings and prosperous cities." This *topos* can be applied to all kinds of bad things. Thus Clement applies it to the wantonness and strife of the Christian community at Corinth. The rhetorical education of the Greeks could be turned to almost any purpose.

4. Livy II.32.8ff. For other ancient authors who tell the same story, see Pauly-Wissowa-Kroll, *Real-Encyclopädie* XV, 840, s.v. Menenius 12.

5. Cf. W. Nestle, *Philologus* 70 (1911) 45f.

6. Clement, I Epist. ad Corinth. c. 20.

7. Eur. *Phoen.* 535ff.

8. Cf. my article on the I Epistle of Clement in *Rheinisches Museum für Philologie* 102 (1959) 330–340, in which I have tried to make some advance in the determination of the nature and time of Clement's Stoic source. On the source problem see also R. Knopf's commentary to the two epistles ascribed to Clement of Rome, in *Handbuch zum Neuen Testament*, ed. H. Lietzmann, Ergänzungsband (Tübingen 1920) pp. 76–83.

9. I Cor. 12.4–11 lists all the different gifts of the Holy Spirit distinguished by the apostle.

10. In I Cor. 12.7 Paul places the emphasis not on the gift (*charisma*) that each individual has been given by the Holy Spirit but on the fact that it was given him to make the best use of it. This distinction between the special virtue or excellence of each citizen and the use he makes of that virtue or excellence for the common good is also found in Greek political thought from the very beginning; it was natural that this problem should be raised again in the early Christian community as soon as serious differences arose.

11. Clement, I Epist. ad Corinth. 37.2–4.

12. James 2.17.

13. The spirit of the Jewish people and its religion as it is understood by Jewish authors is always characterized as that of a law-abiding race that insists on fulfilling the letter of the law with the utmost care. See Josephus, *Ant. Jud.* XVI.6.8f, *Contra Apionem* II.171f.

14. The concept of *synkrasis*, Clement, I Epist. ad Corinth. 37.4, is expanded and elucidated by the following statement concerning the organic relationship of the parts of the body: "The head is nothing without the feet, and so the feet are nothing without the head . . . but *all conspire* (*panta sympnei*) and are *united* in their subordination to the task of preserving the whole body." It seems to have escaped the atten-

tion of interpreters that these words are a paraphrase of the once-famous passage of the Hippocratic book *Peri trophés* (*On Nourishment*) 23: "One confluence, one conspiration, all in sympathy with one another!" This exclamation resounds through the philosophical and medical literature of the late Hellenistic age and the Roman imperial period. This was evidently not due to the direct influence of the little book but to the Stoic philosopher who incorporated in his work both the *synkrasis* quotation from Euripides' *Aiolos* and the Hippocratic passage from *Peri trophés*. We have observed (page 15) that the twentieth chapter of Clement's epistle must be derived from a famous Stoic source now lost. The views of 37.4ff must come from the same philosophical book, because they reflect the characteristic marks of one and the same system of nature. I cannot here give a complete analysis of the vestiges of that Stoic source in Clement, but must reserve this part of the problem to another occasion. But this much is obvious, that Clement has made use of a Greek philosophical theory and interpreted it in his Christian sense in order to give his moral and social appeal to the Corinthians, which he bases on Paul's First Epistle to the Corinthians, 12–13, a strong rational foundation as well. In that regard his approach to the problem anticipates the method of the fathers of the church in the fourth century, who show the same combination of demonstration by biblical authority and of rational argument. Their Christian paideia is not limited to the former but includes the strong element of Greek moral and philosophical tradition that was alive in the minds and hearts of the Christian writers.

15. The last part of Clement's letter apparently sums up the content of the whole. It ends with the great prayer that begins at 59.2. Immediately before this prayer and leading up to it, the speaker makes a last effort to make the Corinthians see his intention without resentment, and it is in this connection that the idea of paideia is introduced. He pre-

supposes the willingness of the Corinthians to recognize the existence of Christian *agapé*: take up once more (he writes) the epistle of Paul the apostle, and understand how the great ideal it holds up to the old unshakable church of the Corinthians has been jeopardized by the shameless actions of one or two people, actions that are unworthy of good Christian discipline. The word *agogé* that he uses here is an old Greek technical term that stresses this special side of a good education. It had often been used of Spartan discipline and self-control. He adds as a further criterion that it means seeking the common good and not one's own interest. That was the much-repeated supreme commandment of classical Greek civic virtue. Clement accepts it, but in the sense of Christian *agapé*; to this he dedicates chapter 49, in which the word is hammered into the mind of the reader in the impressive form of breathless rhetorical anaphoras. Then he once more makes use of that oldest method of Greek educational tradition and gives many examples, of which he merely "reminds" his readers, since they know the Scriptures and pagan history as well (*hypodeigmata ethnōn*).

In chapter 56 the words *paideia* and *paideuo* recur not less than seven times. This continues in the following chapters (57.1, 59.3, 62.3). In the passages in chapter 56 that are taken from the Old Testament, *paideia* has the limited meaning of the Hebrew word for chastisement, but in 62.3 Clement uses the phrase "paideia of God" for the sum total of all the Logia of the written tradition, a use corresponding to the Greek sense of the term. It is used in the same sense in II Timothy 3.14–16. It is obvious that under the influence of the existence of the much-admired "Greek paideia," which was common knowledge for all men, a new concept of Christian paideia was being evolved, the further development of which we are going to trace through the following centuries. The remarkable thing is that this process starts in a group of Christian writings that consists of the Epistles to the Ephesians

(6.4) and to the Hebrews (12.5), II Timothy (3.14–16), and Clement's letter to the Corinthians. Among them the Epistles to the Ephesians and to the Hebrews mark the first steps in this direction, whereas Clement's epistle to the Corinthians shows a large expansion of this idea and of its application in Christian life and thought. The concept of paideia is by no means limited to the "pagan" world of that time but is very much alive among Jews and Christians as well; it is referred to as easily understandable for all, even though Christians and Jews may think they have something of their own to contribute to the question of a true paideia. So the old Greek ideal enters a new phase of its life. History does not proceed by starting with a definition of what it takes over from the past, but by taking possession of it and adapting it to its new purposes .

Notes to Section III

1. Cf. R. Hirzel, *Der Dialog* (Leipzig 1895) II, 368.

2. Cf. Justin, I *Apol.* c. 1; Aristides, *Apol.* init.; Athenagoras, *Suppl.* init.

3. The emperors to whom Justin addresses his *Apology* are called "pious men and philosophers," "lovers of culture" (paideia); cf. I *Apol.* c. 2.

4. Accusation of atheism, cf. Justin, I *Apol.* c. 6. Bearers of the Divine Logos have existed before Christ, see I *Apol.* c. 5.

5. Justin refers to Socrates and Plato in many passages of his *Apologies.* The parallel of Socrates and Christ runs through the entire work.

6. Xenophanes of Colophon, with his violent attacks against the gods of Homer and Hesiod, was the first Greek philosopher who drew the line of demarcation between popular and philosophical theology; cf. my *Theology of the Early Greek Philosophers* [2] (Oxford 1948) pp. 38–54.

7. Justin, I *Apol.* 5.3.

8. Justin, II *Apol.* c. 10.

9. Justin, *Dialogus* 2.3–6.

10. Eusebius, *Hist. eccl.* IV.11.8.

11. Cf. my *Diokles von Karystos* (Berlin 1938) p. 137f on the Jews who were characterized as "a philosophical race" by the early Hellenistic writers and on the source of their information. Later the Jewish religion was called a philosophy, and not only by Hellenistic Greeks: Hellenized Jews had learned from them to see themselves and their religion with Greek eyes. So Josephus, when speaking of the religious sects or parties of the Jews, distinguishes three philosophical schools among them: the Sadducees, the Pharisees, and the Essenes; cf. his *Bellum Judaicum* II.8.2–15, and *Ant. Jud.* XVII.2.4, XVIII.1.2–5. Similarly Philo had spoken frequently of the "ancestral philosophy" of the Jews, or of their laws and customs as the "philosophy of Moses."

12. The long and interesting fragment of Clearchus' dialogue is quoted verbatim by Josephus, *Contra Apionem* I.176. Cf. my *Aristotle* [2], p. 116, and my article "Greeks and Jews," now reprinted in my *Scripta Minora* II, 172ff.

13. Justin the Christian apologist (I *Apol.* 5.4), when he compares the appearance of the Divine Logos in Socrates and in Jesus Christ, says that Socrates revealed among the Greeks what Christ, when the Logos took human shape in him, taught among the barbarians.

14. Cf. Plutarch, *De Alexandri fortuna aut virtute* c. 6. In this famous chapter Plutarch compares the Macedonian king, who unified the nations of the world into one universal state after he had conquered the Persian empire, with the Stoic philosopher Zeno, who, according to Plutarch, set forth the same idea in theory. W. W. Tarn, the historian of Hellenism, misunderstood this passage when he assumed that Alexander is here credited by Plutarch with the political theory of a One-World State. The real meaning of Plutarch's comparison is

that Alexander was something greater than a mere theoretical philosopher when by his deeds he brought into existence what Zeno had conceived only in theory. Plutarch believes that the realization of a great ideal is even more philosophical than its theoretical conception. For the Greeks in general the perfect philosopher is the man who not only possesses true knowledge but who makes practical application of it in his life. From this point of view, Alexander, the man of action, could be called an even greater philosopher than Zeno.

15. It seems paradoxical that nevertheless Philo's works owe their preservation not to the Jewish tradition but to that of the Greeks. However, he was preserved not as part of the secular literature of the Greeks but along with the Greek church fathers and ecclesiastical literature. For Christian theology he was of the greatest interest.

16. Cf. my *Theology of the Early Greek Philosophers*, chapter I, on the concept and origin of "natural" theology in Greek thought.

17. Cf. Aristotle, *Metaphysics* E1.1026[a]10–19, and, on the late Plato, Friedrich Solmsen, *Plato's Theology* (Ithaca, N.Y., 1942).

18. Cf. my *Theology* throughout; that book is dedicated to this special aspect of early Greek cosmological and "physiological" thought.

19. It is taken for granted, and Trypho says expressly (Justin, *Dialogus* c. 2), that he has had a Greek education.

20. The Greek word *xystos* used here by Justin (*Dialogus* 1.1) often means, in the Roman period, a terrace in front of the colonnades of a Roman villa. In classical and Hellenistic times it also signified a colonnade of a gymnasium. This fits the situation in the dialogue better, since strangers like Trypho and his companions would not use the private grounds of a villa for their walks. Cf. H.-I. Marrou, *Histoire de l'éducation dans l'antiquité* (Paris 1948) p. 181, with the reconstruction of the gymnasium of Priene by T. Wiegand and H. Schrader.

21. I have given above only the general sense of the whole introduction of Justin's dialogue. Trypho says (c. 3) literally: "Is not the *whole* endeavor of the philosophers aimed at God, and are not their inquiries *always* concerned with the rule of the universe and with providence, or is it not the task of philosophy to examine the problem of the Divine?" And the Greek philosopher does not deny this, but rather takes it for granted.

22. Tacitus, *Annales* XV.44.

23. M. Aurelius, *Meditations* XI.3. Cf. Folco Martinazzoli, *Parataxeis, le testimonianze storiche sul cristianesimo* (Florence 1953) p. 17f.

24. Ignatius of Antioch, Letter to the Romans c. 4–5, *Die apostolischen Väter*, ed. Bihlmeyer, pp. 98–99.

25. Galen, *De usu partium* XI.14 (*Corpus Medicorum Graecorum* II, ed. Helmreich, Leipzig 1907, p. 158, 2); cf. Richard Walzer, *Galen on Jews and Christians* (Oxford 1949) pp. 12–13 and 32ff. To the well-known passages on Jews and Christians in Galen's extant Greek works Walzer has added some interesting new testimonies from his lost works, which are preserved only by Arabic authors.

26. The references of Galen to the "faith" of Jews and Christians and its place in their "philosophy" are collected by Walzer, p. 14, and discussed p. 48. Walzer aptly cites Lucian's dialogue *Hermotimus* and the philosopher Celsus, another contemporary of Galen, who made the same criticism of the acceptance of "mere" faith instead of critical thought. All three Greek writers reflect the typical reaction of the Greek mind to the Jewish and Christian "reliance" on faith. They all belong to the second century A.D., the time when the rapid expansion of Christianity in the Greco-Roman world was compelling the intellectual leaders of the latter to face the new situation, even though they could see it only through the categories of their own great tradition of a rational culture. They therefore could see "faith" only as a weakness.

27. Tertullian turned against the tendency of contemporary thinkers, both Greek and Christian, in trying to understand "Christianism" as a new philosophy, comparable to the Greek philosophies of the past and measurable by the same logical criteria. "What has Athens to do with Jerusalem," he exclaims, "what the Academy with the Church?" Cf. *De praescriptionibus haereticorum*, ed. Kroymann (*Corpus Scriptorum Ecclesiasticorum Latinorum* LXX, Leipzig 1942) p. 9. On Tertullian's relation to the Greek apologists, whose works he used as sources, see Carl Becker, *Tertullians Apologeticum, Werden und Leistung* (Munich 1954), especially the discussion of the influence of his Greek predecessors (p. 81f) and its limits. Later Latin Christian writers such as Arnobius try to show that faith underlies all human acts and choices and all philosophies as well (*Against the Pagans* II.8–10).

28. The position of Aurelius Cotta, the main speaker of Cicero's *De natura deorum* III, is clearly formulated at the beginning of his critique of the philosophical arguments of Lucilius Balbus (III.2), who has spoken before him. At the end of his long speech Balbus made a strong appeal to him, the next speaker, reminding him of his obligation as the Pontifex Maximus of the Roman state. As such, so it seems, he must welcome the positive attitude of Balbus' Stoic philosophy of religion. Against this admonition Cotta declares that he is indeed ready to defend the Roman religion, but not because he trusts the validity of the subtle arguments of the philosophers. He accepts it as the religious tradition of their ancestors: "cum de religione agitur, T. Coruncanium, P. Scipionem, P. Scaevolam pontifices maximos, non Zenonem aut Cleanthen aut Chrysippum sequor." The names of his predecessors in the high office of first priest of Rome represent what the Latin language calls *auctoritas*. On this basis Cotta can, in the following speech, reject all the arguments of the Greek philosophers for the existence of his gods without endangering his position as Pontifex and defender of the Roman faith. See

my "The Problem of Authority and the Crisis of the Greek Mind" in *Authority and the Individual* (Harvard Tercentenary Publications, Cambridge, Mass., 1937) pp. 240–250.

29. At the end of his *Oration to the Greeks,* c. 42, Tatian introduces himself as the author and gives the name of his "Assyrian" homeland (which, according to the usage of his time, means that he was born a Syrian). He calls himself a professor (*profiteor*) of the philosophy of the barbarians. He was brought up, so he tells the Greek readers of his work, in their paideia, but then he became a Christian. He studied under Justin in Rome, but apparently, despite his great admiration for him, did not share his high respect for Greek philosophy and culture, but was proud to profess a "barbarous wisdom," which he first found when he read the Old Testament. He admired its simple wisdom and language and turned away from the sophisticated rhetorical education and style of the Greeks. But obviously his hatred of everything Greek went deeper than that and had racial reasons.

30. Justin, *Dialogus* 5.6. (This encounter is related by Justin in a dialogue within the dialogue.)

31. Rom. 2.14–16.

Notes to Section IV

1. Acts 17.22.

2. Sophocles, *Oed. Col.* 260.

3. This critique of the old Greek polytheism started with the philosopher Xenophanes of Colophon in the sixth century B.C. According to Aristotle (*Metaph.* A5.986 b21–25), he did not speculate about one single material principle, like Thales, Anaximenes, and Heraclitus, "but looking up to the heavens declared that the one is God." From thence the evolution of the idea of the one God in Greek thought runs from Diogenes of Apollonia through Plato and his school and the Stoic Cleanthes to the theological speculation of the early Roman imperial

age. Cf. my *Theology of the Early Greek Philosophers* and, for the period beginning with Socrates, the older book of Edward Caird, *The Evolution of Theology in the Greek Philosophers*, 2 vols. (Glasgow 1904).

4. See above, page 33f.

5. This applies most of all to the learned commentaries on the works of Aristotle that were written in uninterrupted succession through more than a millennium, ever since Andronicus of Rhodes in the first century B.C. made the first complete edition of Aristotle's *pragmateiai* and thereby became the second founder of the Peripatetic school. It then became a school of commentators.

6. Cicero, *Topica* 1.3, "quod quidem minime sum admiratus eum philosophum rhetori non esse cognitum, qui ab ipsis philosophis praeter admodum paucos ignoraretur."

7. In classical times, when rhetoric was looking for a worthy subject, Isocrates turned to politics. But at the time of the Roman empire, during the first centuries of our era, religion replaced politics as the problem that was becoming more and more of the first importance to the greatest number of educated people. When political freedom was lost, and all that was wanted by the majority was peace and order, the individual found an expression of his inner life and personal liberty only in religion, and he was willing even to lay down his life for his religious convictions — a phenomenon for which it would be hard to find a parallel in the classical age of Greece, though in that age many paid with their lives for their political faith.

8. Origen himself, although a contemporary of Plotinus, the founder of the Neoplatonic school, seems to represent rather the previous stage in the history of Platonism, i.e., Middle Platonism, as Porphyry describes him; for when Porphyry lists the literature on Plato used and quoted by Origen in his lectures, he mentions particularly the authors and titles of that period (2nd century); see page 50.

9. We find this theory already in Philo of Alexandria, who

as a Jewish theologian must have been inclined to accept this version. In the Platonic school proper it occurs as late as Albinus (erroneously called Alcinous in the manuscript tradition), noted representative of the school in the second century A.D. and author of a still extant *Introduction to Plato's Philosophy*. In it this explanation is simply taken for granted; cf. c. 11, in C. F. Hermann's edition of Plato, vol. VI, Appendix Platonica. It is well to remember, however, how much of the Greek tradition of that period we have lost. It seems safe to assume that this interpretation of Plato's ideas originated earlier in the Platonic school and not with Philo.

10. J. Bidez, *La vie de Porphyre le philosophe néoplatonicien* (Gand 1918) p. 34ff. Porphyry later modified some of his views on Plato under the influence of Plotinus, notably his opinion on the question of whether the ideas of Plato exist outside the *Nous* or in the *Nous*. This makes it clear that Porphyry had formed his views on Plato first in the school of Longinus at Athens. That is why, when he later changed them on certain points, an exchange of writings ensued between Longinus and the Plotinian school, including Porphyry himself. The judgment of Plotinus concerning Longinus' quality as a philosopher is found in Porphyry, *Vita Plotini* c. 14. What matters from our present point of view is the fact that the teaching of the classicist Longinus, which began with Homer, was centered about and climaxed in Plato. That was a new kind of classical scholarship. Longinus had received the impulse toward this interesting combination of the literary paideia with the study of Plato and the classical Greek philosophy of the past from Ammonius Saccas, the man who started the school of Neoplatonism and had as his pupils not only Plotinus and Longinus but also the Christian Origen. Porphyry distinguishes another Origen, a pagan who was also a pupil of Ammonius and who published a little. Ammonius himself wrote nothing at all.

11. Porphyry himself wrote a large work in many volumes,

Homeric Questions (ed. H. Schrader, Leipzig 1882), which
J. Bidez would like to place in his Athenian period and consider as a fruit of his studies under Longinus. But even if this
be true, his later turning to a more concentrated form of Platonic studies under the influence of Plotinus at Rome was
hardly a conversion and did not mean his abandoning Homer.
The pupils of the Neoplatonists, partly of Oriental (Near Eastern) origin, needed the study of Homer very badly in order to
understand Plato against his own Hellenic background, as do
modern philosophers. As a matter of fact, Homer was taught in
the Neoplatonic school by Proclus and Iamblichus also, and
could hardly ever have been entirely dropped from it even at
the time of Porphyry, who had written several works on the
great poet. For ages Homer had been the equivalent of what
the average Greek understood by "paideia," as we can see from
the Greek novels written in Hellenistic times. The addition of
Plato expands that traditional concept, and gives the need for
Weltanschauung a central place in late ancient paideia. It is
easy to see that this was both a genuine need and a defensive
measure to counterbalance the growing influence of Oriental
religions like Christianity, which in their education gave religious wisdom the first place. In the earlier history of Greek
paideia Plato had been the first to do that, in his philosophical
way. To him, therefore, they had now to return in order to fill
the gap in Greek traditional education.

Notes to Section V

1. My book *The Theology of the Early Greek Philosophers*
(see note 6 to section III) was written in order to trace the
ideas of God and the Divine and the problems implied in them
back to the earliest origins of such *theologein* in Greek philosophy.

2. Aristotle, *Metaphysics* Λ8.1074 ^{a}38–^{b}14.

3. Aristotle, *Metaphysics* B4.1000 ^{b}9–19.

4. See note 11 above, page 125f.

5. Cf. *Paideia* II, 213ff.

6. We find the shortest and most striking formulation of the reasons that had led to this kind of allegorical interpretation of Homer at the beginning of the book of the so-called Pseudo-Heraclitus, *Quaestiones Homericae*, ed. F. Oelmann (Leipzig 1910) c. 1, pp. 1–2. According to this method of interpreting the Homeric poems, Homer, "to whom we entrust the education of our children from their earliest years," was either the most impious of all men or must be understood allegorically. Plato had accused him of all sorts of blasphemous statements about the gods, but the author of this book thinks that the accusations fall back on Plato himself (cf. c. 4), who did not yet understand the allegoric meaning of Homer's words. In other words, according to Pseudo-Heraclitus, the allegorical method ushers in a new age in which readers with a refined moral taste and purified religious faith will be able to enjoy their Homer again without being deterred by Plato's scruples. Plato had of course not ceased for a moment to admire the poetic beauty of his beloved Homer, but he had questioned Homer's rank as the "educator of Greece," which he saw generally recognized in contemporary Greek paideia. The Stoic critic of Plato's radical rejection of Homer takes the opposite way: he is interested, in the first place, in Homer's role as the paideia of the Greek people, without which Greek culture would no longer be the same. Therefore Plato must be wrong, and Homer must be reinterpreted. The same thing has happened in other traditions, as with Vergil's poetry in later antiquity and in the Middle Ages, the Jewish holy book, the Old Testament, the Koran in the Islamic tradition, etc.; and it has always been at that moment of intellectual development when the literal meaning of the sacred books had become questionable but when the giving up of those forms was out of the question, because that would have been a kind of suicide. The reason for their continuation, but with a different mean-

ing attached to them, was not an intellectual but a sociological necessity having something to do with the fact that the continuity of life depends on form — something very hard for the pure intellect, with its historical blind-spot, to grasp.

7. See the preceding note. In Greek popular religion as represented in the old myths by the poets Homer and Hesiod, the gods often do things that are "not fitting" if judged by the standards of a more developed moral feeling or concept of their majesty. This criticism is voiced for the first time by Xenophanes of Colophon (frg. 26, Diels); see the chapter on Xenophanes in my *Theology of the Early Greek Philosophers*, p. 50. This criterion of the "fitting," applied to the divine being and its supreme dignity, later led to the formation of a special word, *theoprepés*, i.e., "that which is befitting to deity." The problem indicated by this word appears throughout the history of Greek philosophical theology, and so does the word *theoprepés*, which occurs innumerable times in this context. In my book cited above I pointed out the need for a new approach to the evolution of this problem, including its transfer to Christian theology. I was then thinking in the first place of Clement, Origen, and Gregory of Nyssa. In the meantime Harald Reiche, my former pupil, has taken up this task in his dissertation, which, in greatly expanded form, will soon appear as a monograph on the problem of the *theoprepés* in Greek philosophical and early Christian theology. It is in reality the problem of anthropomorphism in Greek philosophical theology and its influence on Christian theological thought, which from its very beginning was confronted with such new issues as the incarnation of God in human form and the concept of the suffering God. Both conflicted with the a priori categories of the theory of the Divine in Greek philosophical theology. It was from such conflicts with Greek ontological thought that the deepest problems of Christian theology were to spring, such as the "Cur Deus homo?"

8. This complex character of Origen has led to diametrically

opposed interpretations of his theological and intellectual character. It is necessary to keep this fact in mind in trying to understand him. The writings of Origen serve different purposes. In his sermons he is addressing the "simpler minds," as he always calls them, whereas in his more learned and philosophical works, such as the commentaries on St. John and Matthew, the *De principiis*, and the *Contra Celsum*, he moves on a higher level. We can hardly explain this by saying that in his sermons we have the true Origen, the theologian of the heart, but that elsewhere he was compelled by his polemics against the gnostics and other pagan critics to make use of philosophical methods of thought and philosophical language. That is what Basil later said of himself in self-defense, but for Origen this was his natural language, in which he felt at home: it was not something assumed for a special occasion or purpose.

This peculiarity has come to be more and more apparent in the efforts of modern interpreters of Origen to grasp the true nature of the great man. Those who have approached him by way of his sermons think that he is in the first place a pious Christian, whereas another group puts the stress on his all-out intellectual effort to apply the entire conceptual means of the Greek philosophical tradition to the great task of creating a Christian theology that could be nothing but a philosophical theology, since that is what the Greek word theology means. But the works of Origen should not be divided in this way and played one against another. They are not an "either-or"; on the contrary, only when they are taken together do they reveal the whole man. The philosophical interpretation of Origen is represented by the great work of E. de Faye, *Origène, sa vie, son oeuvre, sa pensée*, 3 vols. (Paris 1923–1928). Against him, Walter Völker, *Das Vollkommenheitsideal des Origenes* (Tübingen 1931), has argued that for Origen philosophy was a mere methodical instrument, and that the sermons are the principal source of his Christian piety, almost completely neglected by former interpreters. In the sermons Origen appears as a mystic soul, striving for gradual perfection, and as the precursor of later monasticism. In other words, Völker sees Origen against the background of that continuous Jewish-Christian movement of the first centuries A.D. which aims at ethical perfection and leads up to the soul's mystical union with God. Völker's own great merit lies in his analysis and description of that movement, which he traces from Philo via Origen and Gregory of Nyssa down to Pseudo-Dionysius Areopagita. I feel sure that he has succeeded in firmly establishing such a historical continuity of ideas, and has proved a corresponding development of the powerful practical influence of those ideas on Christian life. In this respect Basil and Gregory of Nyssa are inconceivable without Origen's guidance. But when we think of these successors, we may doubt whether they would have understood why this new insight should exclude a true appreciation of Origen's philosophical mind, especially since his followers show exactly the same combination of both constituent elements that we find in Origen; and they always refer to the perfect life as the "philosophical" life. See note 10 below.

9. Porphyry, quoted by Eusebius, *Hist. eccl.* VI.19.5–8.

10. Gregorius Thaumaturgus in his *Oratio panegyrica* (Migne, *PG* X, col. 1069f) tells how his master Origen kept praising philosophy and true lovers of philosophy, saying that only they live a life worthy of rational beings. They alone engage in the right way of life, and they alone know themselves (1069A). What is evident from such words — and one could add many other statements of this sort — is that philosophy was for Origen both *logos* and *bios*, as it was for all ancient philosophers. I suspect that the failure of modern interpreters to recognize the religious capacity of philosophy, in the broad sense in which it was interpreted by Origen, as by Plotinus and Porphyry, is partly due to the fact that for those thinkers philosophy did not have the same meaning as our

modern word but connoted a religion of the spirit. The modern psychology of religion seems to have difficulty in understanding this variety of religious mind, because under the influence of a Protestant concept of faith it has narrowed the field of religious experience and excluded the mind as mere intellect. But such an a priori concept of what "true religion" is would make late ancient religion in its higher forms quite ununderstandable to us, and would limit religion to the irrational. Cf. note 8.

11. These authors, although they represent different types of exegesis, have in common the fact that they always start from the text of ancient thinkers and try to establish its meaning.

12. Cf. note 9. The authors whom Origen used to quote in his lectures, as Porphyry tells us, were mostly those of the school of Middle Platonism. From Porphyry's report in his *Life of Plotinus* we must conclude that Plotinus discussed these same authors in his seminar. They represented the most recent literature about the great philosophers of the past to which both Plotinus and Origen could refer in their interpretation of the classics.

13. See above, note 11 to section IV, page 125f.

14. *Die apostolischen Väter*, ed. Bihlmeyer, pp. 10–34.

15. Cf. Gregory of Nyssa, *In Canticum Canticorum*, introd., where he quotes Origen as the most famous example of this method. There and in his treatise *In inscriptiones Psalmorum* he extends his theory of allegoric interpretation even to the historical books of the Scriptures.

16. *Simpliciores* is the Latin equivalent of the Greek *haplousteroi*, a frequent terminological word in Clement and Origen.

17. Cf. F. L. Cross, *The Jung-Codex* (London 1955). As a first orientation to the entire problem of gnosis, see G. Quispel, *Gnosis als Weltreligion* (Zürich 1951).

18. See Plotinus' book *Against the Gnostics*.

131

19. I shall not quote the entire material to prove this, but mention only Plato's *Symposium*, which in the speech of Diotima describes the ascent of the philosophical soul to the divine suprasensual beauty of the supreme Idea as the successive stages of the initiation rites of a mystery religion; cf. *Paideia* II, 187.

20. Cf. Hippocrates, Law 5 (*Corpus Medicorum Graecorum* I, Part 1, ed. Heiberg et al., Leipzig 1927, p. 8, 15) and *Paideia* III, 11.

21. To give only one example of this, see Clement of Alexandria, *Protrepticus* c. 1-2, a bitter polemic against the mysteries of the Greeks. A look at the index of Clement's work in Stählin's great critical edition s.v. *mysterion* (several pages are required to list the passages in which this and all related words occur) shows the importance of the pagan mysteries for Clement's concept of religion. Christianity is here contrasted with the mysteries of the heathens as the only true mystery. The mysteries are the paideia of the gnostic (*Strom.* VII.1, Stählin III, 6, 8). Their teacher is Christ.

22. I owe this information to Professor Morton Smith of Columbia University, who discovered the new letter of Clement in the library of the Syrian monastery of Mar Saba. He has kindly permitted me to refer to his forthcoming edition of the text and to his commentary on the letter, which he allowed me to read in order that I might form an opinion about its authenticity. So far, he has published only a summary.

23. Cf. note 8 above.

24. Jerome, *Commentariorum in Isaiam prologus* sub finem (Migne, *PL* XXIV, col. 22A).

25. See above, page 10 and note 24 (page 111).

26. See my *Aristotle* [2], p. 54.

27. To see this, read, for example, the first sentences of Clement's *Protrepticus*: they have to be chanted, as was done by the New Sophists of his age, who used certain patterns of rhythmic prose.

28. Melito of Sardis, ed. Campbell Bonner (Philadelphia 1940).

29. The very choice of the title *Paedagogus*, which shows Christ in a new role, points, of course, to the relation of Christianity to Greek culture, since for the Greek-speaking world this was *paideia*, an ideal of human existence to which every educated man and woman and every civilized nation had aspired ever since the idea was launched by the century that produced Plato and Isocrates. The presentation of Christ as the Paedagogus implies a program. What it signifies can be fully understood only against the historical background of the entire Greek paideia tradition; cf. my *Paideia: The Ideals of Greek Culture*, 3 vols. (Oxford and New York, 1939–1944). To see the problem from this angle is clearly something very different from what usually has been done when scholars have compared the Christian writers, and the great Alexandrians in particular, with the Greek tradition. Such comparisons have usually been limited either to matters of literary form or to philosophical content. But when Christ is visualized as "the educator" of mankind, he is thereby contrasted with the Greek idea of culture as a whole, for that is the exact meaning the word *paideia* had developed in the course of its history. The use of the word "pedagogue" in this exalted sense indicates that it no longer means the slave who in the classical centuries of Greece used to accompany a young boy to and from school, but is closer to the philosophical meaning that Plato gave to the word *paidagogein* in the *Laws*, where he defines God's relation to the world thus: "God is the pedagogue of the whole world." This transformation of the meaning and rank of the word was the necessary consequence of the philosophical dignity to which Plato had raised the concept of paideia. And it is this Platonic theological dignity that made it possible for Clement to introduce Christ as the Paedagogus of all men.

30. The Alexandrian learned tradition, especially that of the Jews, had always stressed the antiquity of the wisdom of the

Orient or of Israel, for that was their feeling when they compared it with that of the Greeks. As predecessors they had Hecataeus of Miletus and Herodotus, who were overwhelmed by the impressions they received of the ancient culture of Egypt; and Plato in the *Timaeus* makes the Egyptian priest say to Solon that the Greeks, from his Egyptian standpoint, are always children. On the interest of Plato's Academy in the Orient and on Aristotle's comparison of Plato and Zarathustra, cf. my *Aristotle* ², pp. 131–136. But a systematic comparison of Greek and Oriental wisdom began only in Hellenistic times. The antiquity of the Jewish religion is discussed by Josephus, *Contra Apionem* I.6ff. Justin's and Clement's derivation of Jewish-Christian tradition is only a late echo of this discussion. On Plato as the "Attic Moses" cf. Clement, *Strom.* I.22, Stählin II, 93, 10–11. But it is a bon mot that Clement quotes from Numenius (frg. 9, *Fragmenta Philosophorum Graecorum*, ed. Mullach, III, Paris 1881, 166).

31. Cf. Clement, *Strom.* I.19, Stählin II, 60, 12.

32. Cf. Diog. Laert. I, Prooemium.

33. The Greek philosophers themselves had recognized the so-called liberal arts as the propaideia of philosophy. Now, in Clement's scheme, philosophy itself is downgraded to a propaideia of Christian theology, which is the final gnosis. But only the propaideia (philosophy) comes from man; the true paideia itself derives from God. On the philosophy of the Greeks as propaideia, see Clement, *Strom.* I.20, Stählin II, 63, 8.

34. Isocrates, *Panegyricus* §47ff. Isocrates here attributes to Athens what he calls "philosophia" and "paideia," the ceaseless striving for wisdom and knowledge, and the higher education or culture that is the result of it. From this he derives the possession of "logos," which is what distinguishes the wise from the ignorant. He then concludes from these premises (§50): "And our city has left the rest of humanity so far behind in respect of intellect and speech that her pupils have become

the teachers of them all; the name 'Greek' no longer betokens this particular man but this sort of mind; those who participate in our *paideusis* are called 'Greeks' rather than those who have in common with us only our physical nature."

35. Cf. Plato, *Republic* VI.509b, VII.517b. The Idea of Good is the cause of knowledge and Being.

36. Plato, *Laws* I. 645a-c.

37. Plato, *Laws* X.897b, God is the pedagogue of the whole world.

38. Plato, *Laws* IV.716c. Cf. *Paideia* III, 242.

39. The idea of the divine *paideusis* is of fundamental importance for Origen's whole theology; see Hal Koch, *Pronoia und Paideusis* (Berlin-Leipzig 1932). As is obvious from my picture of Origen, I believe that this book represents a decisive advance in our understanding of Origen's thought. It is true that this Danish scholar's book had its precursors, in so far as others had recognized the profound influence of Greek philosophy on Origen's Christian theology. Such an influence had been demonstrated on many points of doctrine, especially by E. de Faye in his great work on Origen (see note 8). But Koch was the first to put the main emphasis on Origen's idea of *paideusis* and its function in his philosophy of history. It is the idea that gives meaning to Origen's concept of divine providence. Hal Koch has shown the decisive role that these ideas play in Origen's doctrine of the divine plan for the salvation of mankind. Koch's observation of the predominant position of these concepts in the structure of Origen's thought throughout his writings thus becomes the key to the inner unity of Origen's interpretation of the Scriptures. But why has this not been recognized by scholars before? The reason is to be found in a lack of understanding of the central position of the idea of paideia in the historical tradition of the Greek mind at large. This background is lacking even in Koch's own analysis of Origen's theological and philosophical thought. But it is good that Koch arrived at his conclusions from a patient and

extensive reading of Origen's works alone. His results fit most naturally into the whole history of Greek paideia that I have traced from the beginning through the later evolution of this central idea of Greek culture. Origen's doctrine of the divine education of mankind is one of the most striking proofs of the power of that tradition, which thereby enters a new stage of its history.

Notes to Section VI

1. The two highest conceptions of paideia, which transcended by far the trite elementary meaning and practice of this idea, were the two forms that Greek paideia had assumed after the age of the Sophists, in the fourth century B.C. At that juncture, when many foreigners were going to Athens for the sake of "Greek paideia" alone, Isocrates had proclaimed it a universal principle acceptable to all mankind; cf. *Paideia* III, 79.

At the same time Plato had identified philosophy, as he understood it, with the true paideia of man, thereby elevating this traditional concept to the most exalted rank of spiritual dignity; see the interpretation of Plato's *Symposium, Republic*, and *Laws* in *Paideia* II and III. His followers at the time of Origen saw in it their religion. Thus Origen felt that one could understand Christianity on this level as the fulfillment and highest stage of human paideia. He thereby projected it into Being itself and made it the realization of the will of God from the beginning of the world.

2. This makes it easier to understand why St. Augustine keeps referring to Varro's great work, the *Antiquitates*, in his *De civitate Dei*. On Isocrates' religious conservatism, see especially *Areopagiticus* 29 and *Paideia* III, 117.

3. We have referred earlier (page 107, note 6) to this characteristic change of meaning in the word *Hellenismos*. But

the historical situation from which it developed during the conflict of the church and the pagan restoration is quite different from that in the New Testament, where "Hellenes" means those who are not "Hebrews."

4. The emperor Julian excluded Christians as teachers from the schools. He must have seen the danger involved for his cause in the higher cultural aspirations of the Christians, if he took steps to prevent such a development. The State was of course able to enforce his edict, at least for a short time. But in his attempt to restore Greek cult religion and mysteries and to give them a church-like organization, Julian was unsuccessful. His strongest ally was the paideia in the traditional schools, on which he depended; the more enlightened Christian leaders knew this and tried to make use of this weapon themselves.

5. Synesius, *Epist.* 54.

6. Greg. Naz. *Poem. de se ipso,* Migne, *PG* XXXVII. Cf. *De vita sua,* col. 1029ff.

7. Cf. Gustav Przychocki, *De Gregorii Nazianzeni epistulis quaestiones selectae* (Abh. d. Akad. d. Wiss. zu Krakau, Phil. Kl. 1912) and my review in *Scripta Minora* I, 109.

8. Gregory Nazianzen himself soon became an object of rhetorical study and training, and in the same way his poetry was much admired and imitated in Byzantine literature.

9. Cf. Georg Misch, *A History of Autobiography in Antiquity* (Cambridge, Mass., 1951) II, 600–624.

10. On Lietzmann's *The Ancient Church* see the review by Eduard Schwartz, who rightly remarks that the influence of Greek philosophy is underrated in this admirable work. The same is true of C. N. Cochrane's stimulating book *Christianity and Classical Culture* (Oxford 1940), especially his chapter "Nostra Philosophia." But Cochrane is mainly concerned with Latin culture, in which conditions are different from those in the East.

11. Greg. Nyss. *De vita Moysis,* Migne *PG* XLIV, col. 360. Gregory gives an allegorical interpretation of the life of Moses,

after first telling the historical facts; on this exegesis see my *Two Rediscovered Works of Ancient Christian Literature* (Leiden 1954) p. 134ff. The basket in which the child Moses was found floating on the Nile and which kept him above water is the composite classical *paideusis*. Likewise, the fact that Moses was brought up on the wisdom of the Egyptians points to the present great problem of the church: its relation to classical Greek culture. It ought to be used for the "inner decoration" of the church with the *spolia* of the pagans. St. Augustine later adopted both the idea of the high value of classical culture and its derivation from the example of Moses.

12. The little book of Basil always remained the supreme authority on the question of the value of classical studies for the church. It exists in countless manuscripts and has had dozens of editions.

13. *De instituto Christiano*, Greg. Nyss. *Opera*, ed. Jaeger, VIII, Part 1 (Leiden 1952) p. 43, 1–7. The important words are now found in the complete text of the book; cf. my discussion of the text tradition of the *De inst. Christ.* in *Two Rediscovered Works* p. 50ff. The words that refer to the attacks that had been made on Gregory's philosophical theology appear in the *propositio* of the treatise, i.e., in a conspicuous place. Gregory thereby points directly to the defensive aim of the whole work. As I have shown in my book on this treatise, it must belong to Gregory's later years, if it is not his last work.

14. Greg. Nyss. *Contra Eunomium*, ed. Jaeger, lib.III, tom. IX, §59 (*Opera*, ed. Jaeger, II², Leiden 1960, 286, 18).

15. *Ibid.* §52 (p. 285, 19ff).

16. It is characteristic of Gregory's polemic against Eunomius and his followers that he criticizes their Aristotelian logical formalism several times (cf. the index of my edition of *Contra Eunomium*, vol. II, s.v. Aristoteles). I am here using the word "intellectualism" in this sense, as meaning logical technicality, and not in the sense in which some modern critics of Plato have used it in objecting to the Platonic view that knowledge of the Good is the decisive factor in human con-

duct. Cf., for example, Max Wundt, *Der Intellektualismus in der griechischen Ethik* (Leipzig 1907). But Gregory of Nyssa based his entire theology on that kind of "gnosis," i.e., the knowledge of the Good.

17. Greg. Nyss. *Epistulae*, ed. Pasquali, II, §9 (*Opera*, ed. Jaeger, VIII, Part 2 ², Leiden 1959, p. 13f).

18. Gregory never studied at Athens himself, but always calls his older brother Basil his teacher. Through Basil, so Gregory writes to Libanius, the celebrated pagan rhetor of his time (*Epist.* xiii, *ibid.* p. 46, 5–12), he participated indirectly in the rhetorical paideia of Libanius, whose instruction Basil had enjoyed in Palestine (Antioch). On the school of Libanius, cf. A.-J. Festugière, *Antioche païenne et chrétienne* (Paris 1959).

19. Greek education in the schools was at all times based on the exhaustive study of Homer and the rest of Greek poetry. In the Hellenistic age this traditional education, to which the "arts" of the Sophists were added, became a public institution in the cities of the Greek-speaking world. Plato's profound inquiries about the nature of the human mind and the best method of learning had led him to proclaim philosophy the only true paideia; but that did not change the character of the education offered in the public schools. Philosophy remained within the walls of the philosophical schools. The average person was not affected by it. The literary type of higher education thus remained intact even after Plato's time. Cf. H.-I. Marrou, *Histoire de l'éducation dans l'antiquité* p. 223ff.

20. The new Christian literature shows all kinds of literary genres and styles, following the rule of *imitatio* that dominated the activities of the rhetorical schools of the day. Even the Renaissance did not change this later on. The Christian writers all recognize the standard of pagan tradition and taste, but cultivate it in different degrees. The Arian Eunomius, thanks to his artificial diction, of which Gregory in his polemical work against him gives numerous specimens, has gained

a place of honor in Eduard Norden's *Die antike Kunstprosa.* Gregory of Nyssa, who in his way is not less sophisticated than his theological adversary, sees in Eunomius' Gorgianic mannerism a lack of paideia, and even calls his theology *apaideutos.*

21. This gives Gregory a sharply marked position in the history of prose rhythm, and one that sets him off from the rhythmic cadences of classical Greek rhetoric. That he consciously aspired to this distinction, and not only to a position in the history of Christian theology, may seem strange to modern feelings; but it would not have seemed strange to an ancient writer. St. Augustine is the best example of this form of culture, which has often proved offensive to pious souls that prefer simplicity. What makes us unmindful of it is the power of the steady stream of thought, which in turn receives, in addition to its intellectual vigor, the persuasive force of inner passion.

Notes to Section VII

1. The passages in Gregory's works in which the word *morphosis* and its derivatives occur are too numerous for me to collect them all for the modest purpose of this small book. Nevertheless they seem to have escaped the watchful eyes of theological readers, who mostly concentrate their curiosity on points of doctrine only. To the historian of Greek paideia they at once appear as striking confirmation of the unbroken strength of that great ideal, which has upheld the classical Greek tradition even at times when new spiritual sources, such as the Christian religion, were being discovered by the Greek mind and seemed to be transforming everything in man's inner life. *Morphosis,* i.e., the formation of man, is the subtitle of my work *Paideia, Die Formung des griechischen Menschen,* in its original German. In the English edition this was changed to *The Ideals of Greek Culture* because of the

difficulty of rendering the original title literally. But even so, the problem of the *morphosis* of man remains the theme of that work and the root of what we call "humanism." In Gregory of Nyssa Christianity has reached the point where it has drawn its own conclusions from the great Greek experience expressed in the idea of paideia (or *morphosis* of man) — a historical intellectual heritage that history has proved to be "classical" by its effects.

2. Cf. Greg. Nyss. *De instituto Christiano* (*Opera*, ed. Jaeger, VIII, Part 1, p. 44, 27ff). See also *De perfecta forma Christiani* (p. 173ff in the same volume) and Gregory's other ascetic works.

3. Cf. Simonides of Ceos, frg. 37, *Anthologia Lyrica Graeca* ed. Diehl, II (Leipzig 1925) 78.

4. See *Two Rediscovered Works* p. 86ff.

5. See pp. 87–96, *ibid.*, on the problem of "synergy," with the collected passages of Gregory's treatise *De inst. Christ.*

6. Greg. Nyss. *De inst. Christ.* (*Opera*, ed. Jaeger, VIII, Part 1, p. 40, 6ff).

7. Epiphanius, *Panarion* c. 64, ed. Holl II (Leipzig 1922) 729. Origen is there described as "made blind by Greek paideia."

8. Cf. my essay "Die asketisch-mystische Theologie des Gregor von Nyssa," *Humanistische Reden und Vorträge* (Berlin 1960) p. 266ff.

9. *Ibid.* p. 238. The Christian religion is regarded by Gregory as a "way of life" (*bios*), which he calls "the philosophic life" in all his writings. He takes this comparison with other forms of life from the Platonic-Aristotelian tradition and transfers it to Christianity, because during the previous centuries that way of life had taken on more and more a philosophical character, if not for all Christians, at least for the higher intellectual stratum, including the adherents of the monastic ideal. See *Two Rediscovered Works* p. 82.

10. This Greek view of literature as paideia is applied throughout my book *Paideia*.

11. Cf. *Paideia* I, especially the chapter on Homer as educator.

12. Callimachus, the first Greek scholar who wrote a history of Greek literature, or something comparable, gave it the title *Lists [pinakes] of Those Men Who Have Excelled in the Entire Paideia.*

13. On the Sophists of the fifth century B.C. as reformers of the earlier paideia, cf. *Paideia* I, 298–321, Marrou, *Histoire de l'éducation dans l'antiquité*, pp. 81–98. On the development of the *artes*, see F. Ritschl, *Opuscula Philologica* III.

14. On the relation of the *artes* to philosophy, cf. Alois Stamer, *Die ἐγκύκλιος παιδεία in dem Urteil der griechischen Philosophenschulen* (Beilage zum Jahresbericht d. Gymn. Kaiserslautern 1912).

15. Cf. note 1 above (page 140).

16. The most explicit statement of this idea of Christ as the model and of man's participation in him is to be found in Gregory's treatise *De perfecta forma Christiani* (or *De perfectione*).

17. It would be impossible to list here all the passages in the works of Gregory of Nyssa that show this characteristic manner of quoting the Scriptures; they are far too numerous. An *index generalis* of his vocabulary is urgently needed for future work on this Christian thinker. But the task cannot be begun until the critical edition of all his works has been completed.

18. Here the Christian concept of paideia differs from the Jewish idea, which is that Jewish paideia is identical with the Law: cf. Josephus, *Contra Apionem* II.171. The Greeks of the ancient city-state likewise saw their paideia — along with the poets — embodied in the Nomos of the polis. Plato, on the other hand, wrote his *Nomoi* as an expression of his philosophical idea of paideia, as he states in his work.

19. The "Paraclete" is interpreted by Gregory in this paideutic sense. As he comes to the assistance of every individual who pursues the right path, so the Spirit assists humanity as

a whole through a far-reaching adaptation of his language to their limited capacity.

20. In his late book *De instituto Christiano* (*Opera*, ed. Jaeger, VIII, Part 1, p. 42, 17ff) Gregory tried once more to collect all his essential thoughts on the subject (the true *askesis*) that the Holy Spirit "had given us before" (i.e., had given him in his earlier works). We would underrate the personal inspiration of which the great Christian teachers of Gregory's time felt sure, if we attenuated the meaning of this passage and interpreted it as saying "the gifts of the Spirit to all of us," i.e., the common heritage of the Scriptures. The revelation of the Spirit continues in the succession of the apostles and those who took their mandate from them. Similarly Clement of Alexandria speaks with great authority at the end of his *Protrepticus* (Stählin I, 86, 24) in the name of the Holy Spirit, who is speaking through him. Gregory of Nyssa also does so many times, and Athanasius refers to teachers as "God-inspired."

21. See note 15, page 131.

22. Greg. Nyss. *De vita Moysis*, Migne, *PG*, XLIV, col. 360B–C.

23. Greg. Nyss. *In inscriptiones Psalmorum*, Migne, *PG* XLIV, col. 444.

24. Cf. Basil, *In Psalmos* (Migne, *PG* XXXIX, col. 212). Basil begins the introduction to his commentary by pointing out the difference between the paideia given by the prophets and that of the historical books of the Scriptures or the paideia of the Law. The paideia of the Psalms comprehends that which is the most helpful in them all. He compares it with the education provided by medicine, which offers the right treatment for every kind of trauma and disease. As Basil goes on, the reader who knows the *Nicomachean Ethics* of Aristotle is reminded again and again of specific passages in that book, which was obviously standard reading in the philosophical school of Athens. Basil not only shows a good knowledge of it, but from his training in it he arrives at the idea of a Christian

counterpart, which he finds in the Psalms. It will be remembered that Aristotle himself in the Nicomachean version of his *Ethics* keeps referring to the problem of paideia. He was inspired in this by Plato's *Laws*, to which he expressly refers. He occupies an important place in the history of Greek paideia in more than one regard.

25. Gregory of Nyssa, in his book *In inscriptiones Psalmorum*, treats the Psalms in the same way that Basil does, i.e., in a paideutic sense. Basil, who shows a very practical interest in education in his talk on the value of Greek poetry and in the *Rules* for his monks, may have directed Gregory's mind to the whole problem.

26. Rom. 12.2; cf. II Cor. 3.18.

27. Cf. *Two Rediscovered Works* p. 128f.

28. Hence the expression that he uses constantly for the word "God" is "the prototypal (or archetypal) beauty." This is of course God seen in the perspective of Plato's *Symposium*.

29. Cf. Hubert Merki, Ὁμοίωσις Θεῷ (Fribourg en Suisse 1952), with my review of it in *Gnomon*, 1955, p. 573ff (now in my *Scripta Minora* II, 469–481). Merki traces the idea of "assimilation to God" and its transformation from Plato to Gregory of Nyssa.

30. For Gregory, Genesis 1.26 is the link between Christianity and the philosophical tradition of the Greeks. See J. Daniélou, *Platonisme et théologie mystique* (Paris 1944).

31. See *Two Rediscovered Works* p. 110ff, and "Die asketisch-mystische Theologie des Gregor von Nyssa" in *Humanistische Reden und Vorträge* p. 268ff.

32. On St. Jerome's personal acquaintance with Gregory of Nyssa at the Council of Constantinople, where Gregory read parts of his new work, the books *Against Eunomius*, to him and to Gregory Nazianzen, see Jerome's own testimony in his *De viris illustribus* 128 (cf. Jaeger, Prolegomena ad Greg. Nyss. *Opera* II², p. viii). That Ambrose used Basil's *Hexaemeron* in his own work of the same title is a sufficiently established fact and needs no further proof.

INDEX

Acropolis, Renan's prayer on, 3

Alexander the Great, 29, 37; idea of "one humanity," 30, 119; realization of dream, 40; as philosopher, 120

Alexandria, cultural environment, 37; Greeks encounter Jewish religion at, 29–30; Christian school of, 47–48, 53, 54, 56, 57; mystery cults at, 56

Albinus, 125

Allegory, Greek myths interpreted as, 47, 48, 127; Bible interpreted as, 52–53

Ambrose, 101

Ammonius Saccas, 125

Andronicus of Rhodes, 124

Anthropomorphism, Old Testament, 48; in Greek philosophical theology, 128

Antioch, Christian mission at, 6

Antoninus Pius, 28

Aphorisms, ethical, 9

Apocatastasis, doctrine of, 89

Apollinaris of Laodicea, 79

Appollonius of Tyana, 44, 112

Apologists, Greek, 26–29, 34–35, 111; second century, 37; Clement of Alexandria as last of, 57

Apostolic Fathers, 6; literary forms, 7; Didache of the Twelve Apostles, 9; Shepherd of Hermas, 9, 110–111;

Epistles of Ignatius of Antioch, 32; Epistle of Barnabas, 53, 110; Epistle of Clement, see Clement of Rome; "Second Epistle of Clement," 60

Apuleius, 85

Areopagus, Paul's sermon on, 11, 111

Arian heresy, 70, 94

Aristides, Aelius, 44, 45

Aristophanes, 78

Aristotelians, 42

Aristotle, 30, 41, 43, 51, 107; concept of "first philosophy" as theology, 31; attack on Plato's Ideas, 45; on Greek mythology as theology, 47; *Protrepticus*, 59; letters, 79; *Nicomachean Ethics*, 96, 143–144; treatises (*pragmateiai*) and commentators, 124

Arius. *See* Arian heresy

Army, Roman, cited as illustration of unity, 19, 21

Arnobius, 85, 122

Arts, as propaideia, 91

Athanasius, 73, 143

Atheism, Christians accused of, 28

Athens, 3; Paul in, 11, 38; Philip in, 12; Porphyry in, 45; Synesius on scholars from, 76; Isocrates on intellect of, 134–135

Augustine. *See* St. Augustine

INDEX

Aurelius Cotta, 33–34, 43, 122

"Barbarians," Greek interest in religion of, 43

Barnabas, Epistle of. See Apostolic Fathers

Basil of Caesarea, appreciation of Origen, 51, 73–74; education, 75, 76, 77; friendship with Gregory of Nazianzus, 77; writings, 80; famous oration, 81; influence on Gregory of Nyssa, 83, 91, 139; compared with Gregory of Nyssa, 86, 99; commentary on the Psalms, 96; *Hexaemeron*, 144

Barth, Karl, 3

Basilides, 54

Bible, quoted by Clement of Rome, 24; Alexandrian interpretation of, 47, 48; anthropomorphism in, 48, 94; Origen's aim in translating, 49; interpreted by school of Antioch, 52; allegorical interpretation of, 52–53; as Christian paideia, 92–93; as supreme authority, 93; various levels of meaning in, 94–97. *See also* New Testament, Scripture, *and* Septuagint

Brunner, H. Emil, 3

Callimachus, 142

Cappadocia, 75–76, 82, 100

Cappadocian fathers, 51, 52; idea of Christian civilization, 73–75; imitation of Greek culture, 81–85. *See also* Basil of Caesarea, Gregory of Nazianzus, *and* Gregory of Nyssa

Carpocratians, 56–57

Catechetes, school of the, 46

Catechism, oldest Christian, 9

Catullus, 114

Celsus, 121; Origen's controversy with, 37, 49, 58

Christ: messianic message and the Dead Sea scrolls, 4; collections of sayings, 7; as supreme model of submission, 15; analogy of body of, 19; as Logos in human form, 28, 119; translations of sayings, 36–37; portrayed by Clement of Alexandria, 60; as divine educator, 60, 133; as redeemer, 64; Origen's concept of, 66–67; as the physician, 89; and Christian paideia, 93

Christianity, Hellenization of, 5–7; kerygma, 5, 10, 16; early deacons of, 6, 109; sacraments, 9, 28; system of virtues, 16, 87–88; persecution of, 26, 32, 71–72; apologists for, 26–29, 34–35; accusations faced by, 28; interpreted as a philosophy, 29–33; claim to be the truth, 40; theology, 47–49; as mystery religion, 55; cosmology, 63; becomes public religion of Roman state, 70; pagan opposition to, 70–73; concept of divine grace, 88; fourth century humanism, 100. *See also* Literature, Christian

Christianoi, origin of name, 6

Church, mystic idea of, as body of Christ, 19

146

INDEX

INDEX

and Titus), 16, 117, 118; Hebrews, 118; James, 8, 16
Nicaea, Council of, 73
Nicobulus, Gregory Nazianzen's letter to, 79
Nietzsche, Friedrich, 4
Norden, Eduard, 111–112

Origen, 38, 44, 125; *Contra Celsum*, 37, 58, 129; cultural background, 45, 50–51; as founder of Christian philosophy, 46–48; theory of interpretation of the Bible, 47, 49, 52–53, 94; *Hexapla*, 49; philosophy and theological method, 49–50; influenced by Greek philosophy, 50–51, 131; method of teaching, 50, 51–52; sermons, 49, 57, 129, 130; emphasis on gnosis, 54; form of writings, 57–58; scientific books, 58; style of writing, 58; *De principiis*, 58, 129; theological thought, 62–67, 68–69; cosmology, 63; influenced by Plato, 65; concept of Christ, 66–67; use of paideia-concept, 68, 69, 83, 135–136; Cappadocians' appreciation of, 74; contrasted with Cappadocians, 77; compared with Gregory of Nyssa, 86; doctrine of apocatastasis, 89; opposing interpretations of character of, 128–130; as philosopher, 130–131
Origen, the pagan, 125
Orphic tracts, 8, 109–110

Pagan: literature, Christian views mentioned in, 32; wisdom recognized by Paul, 35; opposition to Christianity, 70–73
Paideia: meaning of word, 24; as chastisement of sinner, 24–25, 117; meaning expression of truth (to Plato), 48; Christian religion as, 61; philosophy as, 65; as gradual fulfillment of divine providence, 67; Gregory of Nyssa's conception of, 86–89; meaning Greek literature, 91; Christian, 92–93, 142; Jewish, 142
Paraclete. *See* Holy Spirit
Parmenas, 6
Paul: missionary activity, 7, 10, 11; diatribe in Acts 17, 9; in Athens, 11, 38, 63, 111, 112; letter to Corinthians, 12, 14; cited by Clement of Rome as model of obedience, 15; mystic idea of church, 19; quoted by Clement of Rome, 22; hymn on *agapé*, 22; recognition of pagan contribution to truth, 35; use of allegorical method, 52; speech in Athens, 63, 111; letters of, 96, 109; on metamorphosis, 97–98; impact of Greek philosophy on, 105. *See also* New Testament, books of
Peripatetic school, 124
Persecution of Christians, 26, 32, 71–72
Peter, cited as model of obedience, 15
Peter of Sebaste, 94
Philip, Acts of the Apostle, 11–12
Philo of Alexandria, 7, 9, 119;

151

INDEX

as prototype of Jewish philosopher, 30, 120; justifies Jewish religion to Greeks, 37, 47; *Life of Moses*, 95; interpretation of Plato's Ideas, 124–125

Philology, 46; Alexandrian school of, 58

Philosophy, Christianity interpreted as, 29–33; and theology, 31; teaching of, 51

Philosophy, Christian: founding of, 46–47; precedents, 47–48; fundamental criticism of, 49; and rhetoric, 78

Philosophy, Greek: and parallels with Christian kerygma, 10–12; element of philosophical religion in, 31; evolution of, 41–46; literary forms, 43–44; teaching of, 51; and rhetoric, 77–78; becomes identical with paideia, 91; impact on Christian doctrine, 105–106. *See also* Epicureans, Origen, Plato, Sceptics, Stoics, etc.

Pinax of Cebes, 8, 110

Pindar, 78

Plato, 28, 35, 41, 51; influence on Aristotle, 31; mentions Orphic tracts, 8, 109; and word "conversion," 10; *Timaeus*, 32, 66, 134; second century revival of, 44–46; *Republic*, 45, 48; Ideas, 45, 124–125; meaning of paideia, 48; and Clement of Alexandria, 61; conviction of persistence of "the good," 64, 88; philosophy as paideia, 65, 136; influence on Origen,

65, 66: *Laws*, 66, 98, 133, 142, 144; cosmology, 66; Gregory Nazianzen alludes to, 78; influence on Gregory of Nyssa, 86, 88, 89, 99; rejects Homer as "educator of Greece," 127; *Symposium*, 132, 144

Platonic Academy, 44, 45

Platonists, 42, 43, 47

Pliny, 79

Plotinus, 45, 54, 124, 125; allegorical explanation of Homer, 47; teaching reflected in writings, 51; teachings, 131

Plutarch, 43, 78; *Precepts for Newly Married People*, 8; mention of tracts, 8

Poetry: as basis of Greek paideia, 48; ancient, form praised by Basil, 81, 83–84; Gregory Nazianzen's, 79–80; Greek, idea of divine assistance in, 88; as mold of early Greek paideia, 91

Polybius, 19

Porphyry, 45; *Against the Christians*, 38; *Homeric Questions*, 47; on Origen, 50, 52, 124; views on Plato, 125; *Life of Plotinus*, 131

Proclus, 51

Protagoras, 66

Protreptic activity, 10–11

Psalms, Basil's commentary on, 96, 143–144; Gregory of Nyssa's interpretation of, 96–97, 144

Pseudo-Dionysius, 130

Pseudo-Heraclitus, 127

Pseudo-Longinus, 43

Pythagoras, 35, 55

152

INDEX

Pythagoreanism, 42; way of life, 8; alleged esoteric, 55

Reiche, Harald, 128
Reitzenstein, R., 106
Religious certainty, varying approaches to problem of, 32
Renaissance: fourth century, 75; North African religious and literary, 85; influence of Greek fathers on thought of, 100–101
Renan, Ernest, 3
Rhetoric, 77, 107; Christian philosophy and, 78–80; teachers called sophists, 86; as one of liberal arts, 91
Rome, Greek-speaking Jews in, 20

Sacraments, Christian: baptism, 9; eucharist, 9, 28
St. Augustine of Tagaste, 75, 85, 136, 138; *Confessions*, 80; concept of divine grace, 88; as influence on Erasmus, 101; style, 140
St. Jerome, 58, 101, 144
St. Paul. *See* Paul
Santayana, 39
Satires, 44
Scepticism, heroic, 42
Sceptics, 31, 42
Scripture: Gregory of Nyssa's manner of quoting; 93; anthropomorphic language in, 94; spiritual and educational meaning, 93–97
Septuagint, 7, 24, 30, 109
Sermon(s): as literary form, 7; Origen's, 49, 57; Melito's

Easter, 59, 60; oldest postapostolic Christian, 60
Shepherd of Hermas, The. *See* Apostolic Fathers
Simonides, 87
Simplicius, 51
Sin, problem of, 64
Smith, Morton, 132
Socrates, 10; as prototype of the suffering just, 28; parallel of Christ and, 118, 119
Song of Songs, 52
Sophistic movement, Second (or New), 59, 78, 84, 86
Sophists, 10, 136
Sophocles, 3, 19; *Ajax*, 19, 20; *Oedipus at Colonus*, 38–39
Spirit. *See* Holy Spirit
Stobaeus, florilegium of, 110
Stoics, 7, 31; Paul's sermon to, 11; influence on Clement of Rome, 15, 16; theory of *physis*, 22; teachings on Logos, 28; and problem of religious certainty, 33; system as anticlimax, 41; nonrational religious nature, 41–42, 43; allegorical interpretation of Greek myths, 47; concept of *pronoia*, 67
Symmachus, 71
Synesius, bishop of Cyrene, 76, 79

Tacitus, 32
Tarn, W. W., 119
Tatian, 34, 123
Tertullian, 33, 85, 122
Thaumaturg. *See* Gregory Thaumaturgus
Theodosius, 70
Theology, Christian, 47; prece-

153